The Waterfall of Life

By
Damian Cranney

MAPLE
PUBLISHERS

The Waterfall of Life

Author: Damian Cranney

Copyright © 2025 Damian Cranney

The right of Damian Cranney to be identified as author of this work has been asserted by the author in accordance with section 77 and 78 of the Copyright, Designs and Patents Act 1988.

ISBN 978-1-83538-511-1 (Paperback)
      978-1-83538-512-8 (E-Book)

Cover Images by Damian Cranney

Cover Design and Book Layout by:
    White Magic Studios
    www.whitemagicstudios.co.uk

Published by:
    Maple Publishers
    Fairbourne Drive, Atterbury,
    Milton Keynes,
    MK10 9RG, UK
    www.maplepublishers.com

A CIP catalogue record for this title is available from the British Library. All rights reserved. No part of this book may be reproduced or translated by any form or by any means, electronic or mechanical, including photocopying, recording or by any information storage and retrieval system without written permission from the author.

The views expressed in this work are solely those of the author and do not necessarily reflect the views of the publisher, and the publisher hereby disclaims any responsibility for them.

Summary Review

The book is a collection of poems by Damian Cranney, exploring themes of love, nature, family, national identity, and social commentary.

Reflections on Love and Memory

The poems explore the themes of love, nostalgia, and the passage of time, highlighting the enduring nature of relationships and cherished memories. They convey deep emotional connections and the impact of past experiences on present feelings.

- The writer reminisces about love, emphasizing the lasting impression it left on him.
- The poem reflects on the bittersweet nature of memory in relation to love.
- Love is portrayed as a powerful force that transcends time and circumstances.

Adventures and Quests in Fantasy

This section narrates a knight's quest to slay a dragon, showcasing themes of bravery, folly, and the consequences of underestimating challenges. It illustrates the classic battle between good and evil in a fantastical setting.

- The knight embarks on a quest given by a fairy princess to defeat a dragon.
- He faces various mythical creatures and obstacles.

- The poem serves as a cautionary tale about the dangers of underestimating one's foes.
- Fortunately, the knight triumphed.

Nature's Beauty and Tranquility

The poems celebrate the beauty of nature, capturing serene moments by the sea and the Scottish moors. They evoke a sense of peace and appreciation for the natural world.

- Descriptions of a pebbled beach and a Scottish moor highlight the tranquility of nature.
- The imagery of sparkling jewels and vibrant landscapes emphasizes the allure of the outdoors.
- Nature is portrayed as a source of solace and inspiration.

The Complexity of Family Dynamics

This section humorously reflects on the complexities and challenges of family relationships, acknowledging both love and frustration. It captures the essence of familial bonds and the inevitable ups and downs.

- Family is depicted as a source of both support and annoyance, highlighting the duality of relationships.
- The poem discusses the cyclical nature of family life, from childhood to adulthood.

- It emphasizes the enduring love that persists despite conflicts and challenges.

The Search for Spiritual Understanding

The poems express a desire for a personal connection with God, critiquing organized religion and its intermediaries. They advocate for individual exploration of spirituality.

- The writer wishes to meet God directly, free from religious institutions.
- Criticism is directed at how religions often commercialize spirituality.
- The poem suggests that true understanding of God lies within oneself.

The Nature of Friendship and Support

This section delves into the importance of friendship, highlighting its role as a source of comfort and support during difficult times. It emphasizes the value of true companionship.

- Friendship is likened to a guiding light, providing reassurance in times of uncertainty.
- The poem explores the challenges of maintaining friendships during hardships.
- It underscores the significance of shared interests and mutual care in friendships.

The Impact of War and Peace

The poems reflect on the tragedies of war, the loss of life, and the futility of conflict. They call for reflection on the consequences of violence and the need for peace.

- A soldier's dying moments illustrate the harsh realities of war.
- The poem critiques the motivations behind wars and the politicians who instigate them.
- It emphasizes the need for peace and the lessons learned from past conflicts.

The Joys and Challenges of Fishing

This section celebrates the tranquility and joy found in fishing, portraying it as a means of escape and connection with nature. It contrasts peaceful fishing experiences with the thrill of sea fishing.

- Fishing is depicted as a calming activity that allows for reflection and connection with nature.
- The joy of catching fish is highlighted as a rewarding experience.
- The poem contrasts freshwater fishing with the excitement of fishing in the sea.

The Legacy of Memory and Remembrance

The poems explore the theme of legacy, emphasizing how individuals are remembered by their loved ones. They reflect on the transient nature of memory and the importance of familial connections.

- Everyone is remembered by someone, often for two generations.
- The poem highlights the significance of family stories in keeping memories alive.
- It suggests that even ordinary lives can leave lasting impressions through personal connections.

The Beauty of Nature and Art

The text reflects on the beauty of nature and the ability of artists to capture its essence, emphasizing the connection between humanity and the natural world. It highlights how art can reveal the majesty of nature to those who may overlook it in their daily lives.

- Nature is depicted as a source of warmth and inspiration.
- Artists possess a unique ability to see and convey the beauty of nature.
- The poem encourages readers to appreciate and connect with the natural world.

Environmental Concerns and Action

This section addresses the urgent need for environmental action to protect the planet, particularly focusing on the importance of trees and clean air. It calls for collective responsibility to ensure a sustainable future for generations to come.

- The lungs of the Earth are under threat due to deforestation.
- Trees and plankton are essential for producing air.
- Urges individuals to plant trees and take eco-friendly actions.

Reflections on Life and Aging

The text explores the journey of life, reflecting on the wisdom gained through different life stages and the inevitability of time. It emphasizes the importance of seizing opportunities and confronting challenges head-on.

- Youth is characterized by certainty and confidence.
- Middle age brings maturity and indulgence.
- The passage of time necessitates action and decision-making.

The Complexity of Love and Relationships

This section delves into the intricacies of love, desire, and the challenges faced in romantic relationships. It highlights the tension between physical needs and emotional connections.

- Love is portrayed as a complex interplay of physical and emotional needs.
- The struggle between celibacy and desire is examined.

- Relationships require effort and understanding to thrive.

The Pain of Betrayal and Healing

The text narrates the emotional turmoil caused by betrayal in love and the journey towards healing. It illustrates how love can be both a source of joy and deep pain.

- Betrayal leads to a breakdown of trust and emotional pain.
- Healing is possible through forgiveness and reconnection.
- The impact of love extends beyond the individuals involved.

The Nature of Truth and Deception

This section discusses the human tendency to lie and the consequences of deception. It emphasizes the importance of sincerity and the impact of dishonesty on relationships.

- Lying is a common human behavior with various motivations.
- The consequences of deception can lead to broken trust.
- Sincerity is essential for building genuine relationships.

The Power of Poetry and Expression

The text highlights the therapeutic nature of poetry and its ability to resonate with human emotions. It suggests that poetry can provide solace and understanding in difficult times.

- Poetry serves as a means of emotional expression and connection.
- It can alleviate stress and provide comfort.
- Reading poetry can enhance emotional well-being.

The Legacy of War and Its Impact

This section reflects on the horrors of war and its lasting effects on individuals and society. It emphasizes the need for peace and understanding to prevent future conflicts.

- War leads to loss and suffering, leaving deep scars.
- The text calls for reflection on the consequences of violence.
- It advocates for peace and understanding among nations.

The Role of Friendship in Life

The text explores the significance of friendship and the support it provides during challenging times. It emphasizes the importance of being there for one another.

- True friendship is a source of comfort and support.
- It is tested during difficult times and requires effort.

- Friendship enriches life and fosters connection.

The Journey of Love and Commitment

This section discusses the deep bond formed through love and the desire for lasting commitment. It reflects on the shared experiences that strengthen relationships over time.

- Love is portrayed as a journey filled with shared moments.
- Commitment grows stronger with time and shared experiences.
- The desire for a lifelong partnership is emphasized.

The Struggles of Society and Humanity

The text addresses societal issues such as poverty, war, and the plight of refugees. It calls for compassion and action to support those in need.

- Society often neglects the vulnerable and marginalized.
- The impact of war on innocent lives is highlighted.
- A call for collective action to aid those in distress is made.

Contents

Tom's Mine	18
Family	19
Mad Jasper	21
All The Way	23
Becky	24
Belief	25
Be True You	26
Cry Wolf	27
Jessica	28
Le Bois	29
The Web	30
Belfast Hero	31
Eternal Love	33
Religions Extremes	34
Bleak Fields	35
Life's Road	38
Love's Vicissitudes	39
Red Rum	42

Blue Anchor Bay At Dusk	43
Ruminating	44
Not So Barren	46
The Question	48
The Road Trod	50
The Unlit Road	51
The Female Paradox	52
Cool Rider	54
Finding God	56
Lady Caroline Rothclare	59
Stress Free	61
Love's Needs	63
Look For The Now	64
Seaside Nostalgia	66
For You	68
The Tramp	69
An Exercise In Alliteration	70
Love's Tragedy	71
Love's Rejuvenation	73
The Wife	75

The Soul's Passage	76
Prescribed Poetry	77
Death	78
Dangerous Seas	79
Let The Earth Breathe	80
Go Fishing	81
Life's Road	83
You Are My Love	84
Can I Buy Some Happiness Please?	85
Date With A Vampire	86
Lying Not Standing	87
Forgive You Your Sins	90
An Independent Scotland (Or, Beware The English)	91
Two Lives Together	94
Don't Vacillate	95
The Tallyman Of Life	96
A Life In Shadow	97
We Hope You Stay But If You Go	98
In Between The Light And Dark	100
Cast Off Your Shrouds	101

Wide Sad Eyes	102
In Memory Of	103
The Crack	104
A Pebbled Beach	106
A Vote For Freedom	107
Independence Day	108
A Place Without A View	111
A Chance Encounter	112
Nature's Design	113
The Babs Of Koth	114
The Man In The Dock	116
Bubble The Rat	118
War Graves Visit	119
The Orb	120
The Powers That Be	121
Scotland Be Brave	123
Spectral Dream	125
The Ex-Soldier - An Allegory	126
A Scottish Moor	129
The Knight With No Name	131

England	133
The Rape Of Poor Greece	135
Hidden Evil	138
Friends In Your Life	139
The Soul's Progress	141
Duties Reward	143
Snowdonia Walks	148
Fickle Fate	150
Follow That Stream	152
The End Of The Pier	154
Shield Of Truth	157
To Fly Like Birds	159
Reasons For Drinking	160
Love's Lost Time	162
Who Cares! Have A Beer	164
They Had No Choice	165
The Lie - Or Is It Alright To Tell A Little White Lie?	167
Coming Of Age	169
Out Of Time	170
Water	172

Parky Benders	173
The Strength Within	174
Free Moments In Time	175
Peace On Earth	177
Shield Of Truth	178
Steam Travel	180
Agincourt	183
Excuse For War	185
A Buzzing Bee	187
Rabbit	189
Duel Of Death	191
The Undefeated	195
Take No Care For Tomorrow	197
One Man's War	198
Where have all the wise men gone?	200
Daniel Cretona	202

Tom's Mine

The soldier bravely trod the sod,
The sod he chose to tread was fine,
Until he trod upon a mine,
-His apparel was left in disarray,
Because he chose to die that way!

Hold on, I hear you say or sigh,
He did not choose that way to die,
It was his duty, he had no choice,
But I listen to that little voice,

If you would listen like I do,
You would also hear it too,
It whispers, if he'd stayed at home,
Into pieces he would not be blown.

And if the other million men,
Who took up arms had stayed in bed,
And told the man in grey and khaki,
That they found all war a bore,
And would they go and knock next door,

There would not have been a bomb,
To sink beneath the sod for Tom,
And our brave soldier would not say,
"I got blown up by mine today."

2011

Family

Family, family, why on earth do we have one,
They make you feel wanted but also quite put upon?
We wouldn't be here, if they'd not been there,
But if they weren't there, with whom would you share?

We love most of them dearly, but would you not say,
They drive you all mad in an annoying mad way,
They bicker or banter all day at each other,
And then put the blame on their sister or brother.

Now don't get me wrong, I love them, I do!
But, it's a bit like wearing, an uncomfortable old shoe,
And like that old shoe, that is crinkled and worn,
You have to replace it, and another one's born.

The new family member, is loved and adored,
Quite rightly, they should be, I am in full accord,
But they morph into teenagers, sullen and grim,
And blame you; for all of the problems, they're in.

When puberty's done, and the hormones are calmer,
And you think you'd quite like, a holiday in Palma,
They then become adults, and you think that at last,
The problems are over, and are now in the past.

The Waterfall of Life

You're kidding yourself, of course they're not finished,
The hopes of that holiday, are more than diminished,
'Cos, the children, all have, their own problems to share,
And you can't ignore that 'cos you care, you care.
Let's face it, for them, you'll always be there.

May 13, 2011

Damian Cranney

Mad Jasper

She walked in beauty Spare and Sprite,
While all around her stopped and stared,
As if in awe at such a Sight,

But on she moved, oblivious She,
To those that Stared but could not see,
That now at last she could be free,
From Jasper's mad chicanery.

She had a goal, that she would follow,
To rid herself of that foul fellow,
That would right the wrong that Jasper's greed,
To those she loved, and to whom she cleaved,

Had caused such pain, and hurt her brother,
If not for him then for her Mother,
Mad Jasper must be seen to suffer.

It was only the next day that she saw,
That all her plans were made of straw,
Mad Jasper had the right of might,
And could with her win any fight,
But then suddenly to her delight.

The Waterfall of Life

He rang up and apologised,
He'd been a fool and realised,
He needed her more than any prize,
And that the national lottery voucher,
Which she had bought when he was with her,
Was hers to keep if she would only,
Give him back, his walkman Sony.

She thought and weighed the cost and balance,
They had won ten pounds in the game of chance,
The player was worth considerably more,
She just texted back, 'go away you bore',
Revenge is sweet, she had dealt the blow,
That brought the bad Mad Jasper low.

May 13, 2011

Damian Cranney

All The Way

I met her just after she finished at school,
I'm not by nature a silly old fool,
But it's now been forty years since then,
So I need to write down how, feel with a pen,
I love her now more than ever I guess,
And I know that without her I'd be in a mess.

The years have gone by, looking forward to spending,
growing old together, in bliss never ending,
We've always been there looking after each other,
She nags me of course, But more like a mother,
Who tells her child off because she wants him to be,
Like the man she once knew, that used to be me.

And now I arrive at the end of this missive,
And, I don't mean to sound as if I'm dismissive,
But no one knows how strongly she copes,
With this illness I have which has dashed all our hopes,
Now please understand this is not a sad letter,
We still love each other and mucking together,
Will fill every day with as much as we dare,
And never take lightly 'the love that's still there.

May 13, 2011

Becky

Becky, my Becky, our Becky,
She's lovely in spite of herself,
She'd frighten a big hairy yeti,
Yet charm you right off your shelf.

By nature vivacious and pretty,
An off-key songbird that's witty,
But like Churchill who had his Black dog day,
She sometimes feels bad in a sad way.

We know that she's loving and caring,
But takes offence at your standing a-staring,
Just give her a smile. Wait just for a while,
And she'll make you feel better by more than a mile.

Belief

There has been a tragedy in my life,
And no, it's not my lovely wife,
And if it was, I would not say,
Because I'm still alive today,
And planning to remain that way.

No the tragedy is, I have to admit,
I no longer believe in religion's remit,
We all have a need to know why we're here,
And it's the not knowing, that most people fear.

It's ironic to me that as I grow older,
I face my mortality like an old soldier,
Not giving a damn, about fire and damnation,
Which nurtured by church and the invention of Satan,
Admittedly made me a boon to the nation,
But I find I'm still good, in spite of the fact,
That religion is only a theatre act.

My thoughts, if you want them, if not read no further,
Those Religions are started, by this one or that,
Who make up the rules picked out of 'a hat'?
If you want to find God, or believe in a force,
Then you have the answer, it's within you of course,
If you want to be social, then go join a club,
As for myself, here's to you, I'm off down the pub.

May 13, 2011

Be True You

In seasons past the fustian class,
That is those who toiled and broiled,
Would always bear truth,
To the faults of their youth,
As an example to those that do follow.

But in the current climate of me,
The self can no longer admit it or see,
That the weakness itself, is not to declare,
That fault can be cleansed by admission,
But the id will not risk that derision.

May 13, 2011

Cry Wolf

There was a young Cestrian youth,
Who found difficulty telling the truth,
It happened so often, his friends had forgotten,
To give credence to anything he said;
Then one day he needed, them all to believe him,
He found that he needed a pound,
His lies had preceded, the belief that was needed
For confidence at this request,
His friends they just sniggered, he found himself jiggered,
And no one was found, who would lend him that pound.

May 13, 2011

Jessica

Jessica with the smiling face,
Reflecting all my grandma's grace,
Reminding me of my mother's charms,
I love to hold you in my arms.

Your mother was my darling girl,
When she was born the world did whirl,
Now that you are here, my dear,
The circle is complete and clear.

Each generation blends together,
The daughter then, is grandma now,
This baby girl will one day be,
Mother of the family tree.

May 13, 2011

Le Bois

In meadows full of rolling green,
A far-off wood completes the scene,
It stands atop the distant brow,
And fills my heart with warmth, somehow.

In England there will always be,
Vistas of uncertainty,
That then are turned to Majesty,
By those blessed with the gift of seeing,
Becoming one with nature's being.

Many artists have been fortunate in this,
That they possess insight into the abyss,
Whilst most people view but still cannot see,
They make it so easy for you and for me,
To view all of heaven in nature's beauty.

May 14, 2011

The Web

The web as we know it, is a marvellous tool,
It doesn't matter if you're a genius or fool,
You can use it for info, for stealth or for guile,
And become totally addicted in a short while.

Love it, or hate it, the web's here to stay,
I personally think it's a great way to play,
It also completes 'The phenomenon of Man',
And 'Complexity consciousness' of Teilhard Chardin.

The web is a means of human integration,
Bringing people together from every nation,
We can all have a say in what happens to us,
Together we'll make a world syllabus,
And the strength of that idea is gaining apace,
For the web is now linking the whole human race.

May 14, 2011

Belfast Hero

Let me not be first in anger,
Cool and calm shall be the rule,
He who loses self-control's in danger,
Of being made to look a likely fool.

I remember once in Bangor,
Where the Bay of Belfast sits,
An angry man who could not conquer,
his nature's dark and adverse fits.

He was walking by the quayside,
Having drunk his fill in ale,
And a dram or two in whiskey,
All added to this sorry tale.

A fisherman who had all day,
Been battling nature's wildest sea,
He'd finished work and on his way.
Was homeward bound for wife and tea.

The drunken man who would not see,
Anything else, but an enemy,
Chose quite unwisely to berate,
The seaman who by now was late,
For home and hearth, and dinner plate.

I needn't tell the whole sad tale,
The angry man was sent to jail,
The happy bit, I will just mention,
The seaman as is the convention,
Became a hero in the press,
And, was feted by the mayor no less.

Eternal Love

My love for you could die a death,
That is if it was small and weak,
And could not stand a test of strength,
But it is strong and full of fire,
And with it to the highest peak,
or to the farthest length of length,
It could for you face any test,
To its utmost point but nothing less.

Yes nothing less for you would do,
But the most my body could give,
And I do not mean my body alone,
My heart, my soul, my spirit
Are yours for longer than I live,
And when the quick of life is gone,
We'll be together, two souls as one,
Perfect love in heaven's infinity,
Loving each other for all of eternity.

July 22, 2011

Religions Extremes

Religion is only an invention by man,
An attempt to explain the universal plan,
As a set of rules, it sometimes can be,
A way of living in harmony.

However, it always engenders in man,
A partisan instinct, which makes him then hate,
Anyone with a different opinion to state.

Should any one suffer, from religions extreme,
Or in God's name, because of this theme,
Then religion is obviously, not part of the plan,
Is it possible to justify? Try if you can.

But if you participate in justification,
You're part of the problem of harmonisation,
Your feelings are all full of good intent,
But more is required, if dissent, you would prevent.

The greatest precept for living your life,
Is that which adjures you to treat others,
As you would want to be treated yourself,
If everyone practised that dictum,
Then Religion could be left on the shelf.

April 9, 2012

Bleak Fields

In a cold bleak field,
a soldier lay dying.
There were others around him,
Who also were crying.

The medics risked all,
To try to gain ground,
But the incessant chatter,
Of maxims and Mausers.

That chewed up the grass,
And the mud all around,
kept the bravest of brave,
From risking his trousers.

Or stop the dying from living,
or their mothers from sighing,
In no man's land, the dead did lie,
With vacant stares up to the sky.

There have been so many,
Wars since then,
And it always requires,
The death of brave men.

The brave politicians,
Of course take great risks,
A successful conflict,
Can enhance their career.

But if it goes wrong,
He might lose that post,
That would give him,
An extra big pension to boast.

He certainly won't have,
To think about death,
In a field were those young men,
Gasp out their last breath.

Whatever happened to,
The war, to end wars,
A whole generation swore,
That never again,

Would nations commit,
To a spurious cause,
Were their young lie dead,
Before they were men.

But people are all,
Very easily fooled,
By hatred and lies,
Their perspective is fuelled.

Remember this principle,
And use it to judge,
The cause is not right,
If there's anyone dead,
From the rhetoric that,
We have all been fed.

April 15, 2012

Life's Road

When in my youth I knew the truth,
To all of life's stark questions,
With flippant ease, to please or tease,
I had the answer, could seize the day,
Was sure of myself, in every way.

When in the middle years of life,
I matured a bit, could take advice,
The world was still all mine to conquer,
But it didn't matter now, if it took a little longer,
Diverted by indulgence, in the luxuries of life,
Whilst coping with the problems of daily toil and strife.

Now comes the rub, time ticks its knell,
Good intentions, will pave our own road to hell,
And all those things that we thought could wait,
Chances are that we probably, have left it too late,
You can change it of course, it depends on how well,
You react to this warning, only you can tell.

So let us stop tempting, the arbiters of fate,
Grasp life by the throat, and not hesitate,
We have it within us, to map our own course,
The route may have to be taken with force,
But obstacles are only problems not solved,
Just meet them head on until all is resolved.

May 9, 2012

Love's Vicissitudes

Our spirits sometimes,
Meet as one,
l will love you till all,
The seas are gone.

But my need for you,
is more than ethereal,
It stems of course from,
parts quite cerebral,

But manifests down to,
parts that are physical,
And the lust of the body,
Takes over the spiritual.

When age creeps upon us,
your thoughts are the same,
As when, as a young man,
You were always game.

to play the field wildly,
With any cute thing,
You're now an old roué,
If you fancy a fling.

The Waterfall of Life

Back then it was,
nudge, nudge he's a bit of a lad,
In your head you're no different,
It's all rather sad.

Who cares, when we love,
The world doesn't matter,
Mouths wantonly roving,
Prohibiting chatter.

Entwined in embraces,
And fluid exchanges,
Exploring our bodies,
Like mountain ranges.

Clambering heights,
We have not dared before,
Let's go to the edge,
And together we'll soar.

Last night I dreamed that,
We did just this,
I awoke from this tryst,
In an ecstasy, of bliss.

And then in joyful love,
My waking found,
It was no dream,
How my heart did pound.

Because I knew that,
You were there,
Loving me, more than,
I could hope or dare.

November 10, 2012

The Waterfall of Life

Red Rum

Red Rum was pounding the turf down at Aintree,
Going as fast as any horse can be,
Ginger was there looking on at the side,
And the whole of Liverpool, filled up with pride.

For the third time now, this great horse had won,
The greatest steeplechase under the sun,
At Aintree a horse is more likely to die,
For the third time Red Rum, the odds did defy.

Around the world the bookies all suffered,
The betting fraternity knew they weren't buffered,
To lay off a bet when the horse is a hero,
Is not easy, so most, were left with a zero.

The ordinary punter, who fancied a flutter,
Even, the tramp, who lived life in the gutter,
Joined with the housewife who bet the housekeeping,
On the horse with the heart which always kept beating,
Because they all knew Red Rum would win through.

November 12, 2012

Blue Anchor Bay At Dusk

We strolled the beach at Blue anchor bay,
enthralled at the scene as we made our way,
The sea and the sand were bathed in gold,
from the rays of the sun as the day grew old.

Down the beach dogs and people ambled quite slow,
Silhouetted, against the reflected sun's glow,
A little girl and her mum were digging,
for crabs, or maybe, were sandcastle building.

Upon a far ridge Dunster castle was there,
Like a mirage it hovered as if in mid-air,
The scene was just magical and so I took this,
A picture, in order to just reminisce.

December 18, 2012

Ruminating

I can do obtuse,
Said the rhymer to blank verser,
I can reference classical,
Be Keatish and elitist.

But I would much rather ruminate,
upon the penultimate,
In words that illuminate,
The subject to disseminate.

Having patronised the writer,
whose verse is that much lighter,
I would have to say, the Scribbler,
Excelling in blank metre,
Lends gravitas, to the spoken word,
As acted in the theatre.

Let's not forget,
there's room for all,
who love the written word,
Write down the prose,
The rhyme or verse,
And let it all be shared.

Both Milton and Shakespeare,
did the ultimate with blank,
Because they both had genius,
It is them, we have to thank,

The nursery rhyme has merit,
in engendering in the young,
A love of rhyming couplets,
Especially, when they're sung.

December 18, 2012

Not So Barren

Upon the barren rocks, I stood,
and gazed far out to sea,
And watched white horses, racing in,
to dissipate in frothy spew, against the craggy lea.

The raging clouds, the pregnant pause,
Waves, bursting, in tempestuous force,
More followed and it seemed to be,
increasing in ferocity.

Though frightening, in its aspect,
And as the wind chill blew,
Nature's seeming wildness,
brought order to the view.

I could have stood for hours,
a witness to the scene,
But life and strife, plus distance ran,
forbade I Stand and Stare.

I will return, I will come back,
But now off home, to those who care,
Warm greetings and a fiery hearth,
For tea, some ham that's lean.

Damian Cranney

A cuddle from the wife is nice,
And so is your own arm chair,
To snooze contentedly the while,
you dream of where you've been.

The Question

I've asked this question before,
but I'm going to ask it once more,
If religion is right and your God has the might,
where is the need to bicker and fight?

How strong is the faith you subscribe to?
If it's strong then it needs no defence,
If the message it sends is divine,
it will be seen as being sublime.

If someone insults you, don't be so intense,
To feel you should kill him, it doesn't make sense,
And God, in his wisdom, will not take the blame,
For you using his name, in the killing game.

You cannot be more insulting to God,
than to take a life, that he has created,
For religion's sake, is the excuse that you make,
but that is just belated.

And we both know, that man is dead,
Because he is someone you hated,
If religion espouses hatred and death,
Those doctrines came not from God's sweet breath.

Damian Cranney

Has religion represented God well on earth,
The Creator of all, since man's first birth?
Well Cromwell massacred the Irish,
Sinn Fein killed 3000 up north.

In Gujarat, many Muslims were killed,
by Hindus I think you will find,
The Armenians were slaughtered by Turkish forces,
At the time, no one seemed to mind.

The biggest massacre, the holocaust,
should never ever be forgotten,
Or else mankind is condemned to be,
forever truly rotten.

And it is from those who survived,
That a nation in hope, was derived,
If that hope can be shared for the good,
And all aspirations are mutually understood.

Then the hopes of a people who are just like you,
And if for a moment, you balance all points of view,
The Palestinian aspirations are easy to see,
they just want control of their own destiny.

May 27, 2013

The Road Trod

l look in the mirror and what do I see?
Some old man, stood staring, looking back at me,
Where is the light that shone from those eyes?
That made dreams so easily materialise.

Whatever happened to that daring young buck?
Who made things happen, without counting on luck,
Well, l still make things happen and I always will be,
In control of my future and my own Destiny.

I don't believe in might have's, what if's, and if only,
the road I've trod, has never been, the least bit lonely,
l don't regret, a single act or road that I have taken,
The only important thing to me, was bringing home the bacon,
I will apologise, to those, whose toes I may have broken,
As apologies go, I fear this is merely token.

May 31, 2013

The Unlit Road

Let explorers go where they will,
I have discovered my paradise in thee,
New worlds do not me, with interest fill,
For you have set my roaming spirit free.

Of distant lands I dream no longer,
And I cannot think of elsewhere being,
As my passion grows, the bonds get stronger,
Your presence blesses me with seeing.

You light up the road, I now must follow,
Before you were there, the road was dim,
But anywhere, without you, would be hollow,
And parting, be it but an hour, is merely an interim.

June 10, 2013

The Female Paradox

The enigma that is woman,
Intrigues the mind of man,
But there are many dangers,
In this universal plan.

The company of women,
we all agree is fun,
Man struggles however,
when he loves but only one.

She smiles upon you brightly,
That smile outshines the sun,
You take it for a green light,
you should have just stayed dumb.

You spend a lifetime, learning,
how to please, the hard to please,
You think you've got the hang of it,
and then, you're on your knees.

But life would be so boring,
If you knew just where you stood,
And when she says it's you she loves,
It makes you feel so good.

Damian Cranney

That doesn't happen often,
Or complacency would rule,
So the game of what she's thinking,
Still dominates your thoughts.

So be careful if she asks you,
"In this do I look cool?"
It's a trap set for the wary,
Make sure you don't get caught.

If only you could have a guide
On the rationale of women,
But no one is there brave enough,
To pen that contradiction.

The contradictory nature,
Of the female by your side,
Does not mean, you are immature,
Don't let it dent your pride.

A man's place is in the wrong,
I think I have that right,
At least that's what she told me,
Just the other night.

Poetry paradoxically,
Man finds to be sublime,
He can eschew, the logical view,
And express himself in rhyme.

June 15, 2013

Cool Rider

He rode into town, with an easy grace,
On his horse, at a leisurely pace,
He didn't slow down, he didn't look round,
The street was deserted, and he heard not a sound.

The silence was eerie, but then it was broken,
A woman ran into a house with her child,
And a dog started barking nearby,
Scaring two birds who flew into the sky,

He tethered the animal outside of the bar,
Stepped up to the doors, and pushed them ajar,
Walking into the dimly lit room he could see,
A saloon full of men, drinking rye whiskey.

For a moment the whole place went silent,
As he walked to the bar with intent,
The bartender looked him straight in the eye,
What'll it be he said, can I pour you a glass of rye?

"That's very kind," he said, "I've ridden hard today,
Pour me a long cold drink of milk," the barman heard him say,
Someone in the crowded room, could not restrain a snigger,
And a ripple of laughter started and gradually grew bigger.

The barman said, "Yes sir. Cold milk, did you say?"
Our man stayed cool, it just was his way,
He ignored the laughs, he just let them pass,
They stopped when he said, "Yes milk, but in a dirty glass."

June 25, 2013

Finding God

I would like to find God,
The enquiring mind said,
But I don't really want,
To have to wait till I'm dead.

And when I say find him,
I do not mean in spirit,
If he really exists,
I would like to pay him a visit.

I would like to be able,
To ring up and say,
Is it ok if I call round,
And see you today?

I believe we are made,
In his likeness, they tell,
So if he's like me,
We should get on quite well?

Now please understand,
I am not being blasphemous,
I would love to meet God,
With no church in between us.

Damian Cranney

By church I mean all,
Of the third party religions,
Who like business are franchised,
In all of the regions.

The simile with business,
Is very compelling,
Each religion treats God,
As if they were selling.

And to compete in that market,
They have to state,
They own exclusive rights,
To God and his fate.

To ensure you don't stray,
Or deviate from their path,
You follow their way,
Or you incur God's wrath.

And no matter how good,
Your intentions might be,
You're "with them or against 'em,
Or condemned eternally."

The Waterfall of Life

If there's only one God,
And he's common to each,
Why should you believe,
What those religions preach?

I still think that my way,
Would be better by far,
And him being omnipresent,
I don't even need a car.

June 27, 2013

Lady Caroline Rothclare

She was bad, cunning, pretty and bold,
And her story I must tell before I get old,
Her father an Earl who fell on hard times,
Turned rogue and then was hung for his crimes.

She was brought up a Lady, thought everyone fools,
Was devoid of scruples, and obeyed no rules,
She could fence, shoot, and out ride any man,
Reeking revenge, her reason to live and plan.

Two men she blamed for the family's woes,
Both would be seen writhing in death's last throes,
The first, Lord D'arcy, an effeminate young buck,
Cheated her father at cards, he was now out of luck.

Confronting him at Boodles, exclusive gaming club,
In male attire, shocked members were, like rats in a tub,
Her verbal wit he could not match, her challenge he accepted,
He died at dawn, she ran him through, her skills he underrated.

Lady Caroline Rothclare, her vengeance she would follow,
But she needed money, or all her plans were hollow,
Dressed in black, she wore a mask, a pistol adorned each hip,
And many a highway coach was robbed by her daring Ladyship.

The Waterfall of Life

The second man she blamed the most, a banker without heart,
Extension to her Father's loan, he would in no way part,
She was of course not right to take this evil point of view,
But hatred blinds our thoughts and so she killed him too.

I would like to say, her evil ways were punished by the law,
But her life was long and happy and eventually she saw,
that life could be much better, if she turned her back on crime,
And now she very rarely robs, she just doesn't have the time.

October 15, 2013

Stress Free

I walked amidst the shadows,
that curtained life,
I looked for the sun,
to relieve my pain.

If you had been with me,
it would have released the hurt,
But you were absent,
when my need was great.

It does not matter now,
I know that how,
I am comforted by your presence,
Beside me.

l live each day for each day,
And you, my love.

The time is near,
When my absence may hurt you,
But dwell not on that,
but on what we have been.

And if in future times,
you need a love,
I will smile on your need,
And bless you.

May 8, 2014

Love's Needs

Yield not your favours maiden mine,
At least not until the end of time,
It is important that you keep,
Your body pure so you can sleep.

Unfortunately my tenure here,
will not support so long a fast, l fear,
So with a heavy heart l must pursue,
others less principled in their view than you.

I doubt I would enjoy such trivial liaisons,
But physical needs create unsavoury occasions,
My heart and needs respect your zealous grace,
But conscience is dumb, in passions strong, embrace.

Of course I would eschew all thoughts of tawdry bliss,
If from your honeyed lips I could draw one kiss,
In gloried celibate state, for a while I would repine,
But not of course forever or until the end of time.

May 8, 2014

Look For The Now

As we pass along life's path,
coasting towards the end,
of what has been,
and what has still to be,
will spiritual release, be granted to all,
or is our heritage to be just dust,
in a vacant eternity?

I have walked in hope,
I have laughed and cried,
I have seen despair around me,
But there is always someone near,
some help in life's dark mire,
who fill the void with kindness,
Reawakening life's cold embers,
into a warming fire.

Searching for the why,
looking for the way,
the answer will be found, for sure,
but not I fear today.

Lucky are those who live,
and question not,
Following others who know not
Having faith in a journey
Whose destination is not known
hoping to arrive at their spiritual home.

Which prophet to follow?
So many to choose,
There's Christ and Mohammed,
and Abraham too.

Vishnu and Bhudda represent many,
Indeed India had more than any,
China has now, but only a few,
Ancient Pantheism once was rife,
maybe that is the meaning of life.

Keep looking, keep loving, keep living,
Death might be the only reward!

May 8, 2014

Seaside Nostalgia

As I wandered free and easy,
all along the sandy shore,
Dipping toes into the sea edge,
listening to the tidal roar,

Surrounded by the sounds of summer,
heated by the sun,
Noisy, strutting seagulls eating,
Laughing children having fun.

I came upon a Punch and Judy,
loud and raucous, puppet show,
Fond memories of a childhood stirred,
Is it that long ago?

Oh no! it isn't Punch, said Judy,
Oh yes! it is, the kids replied,
It's right behind you they insisted,
hurry! hurry! go and hide.

Donkey rides, passed by,
and as I reached the pier,
I thought, I'll have an ice cream,
or perhaps a pint of beer,

Damian Cranney

for tea some fish and chips,
before it gets too late,
A day out at the seaside,
is nostalgia on a plate.

May 8, 2014

For You

Ask me why and I will find the answer,
Ask me the way and I will guide your footsteps,
Question the reason and I will justify the action,
If you are worried, I will be beside you,
If you need me, I will be there for you
If you need comfort I will hold you,
If you need love, I will love you,
If you need to love I will caress you,
I will not make demands on you.

I am there by your side whenever you need me,
Your presence uplifts me,
Together we are as one,
Without you, life is empty,
But with you, life is fun.

Now and forever,
Always in tune,
Hold my hand now,
And I'll take you to the moon.

May 8, 2014

The Tramp

I need to change my life, the tramp was heard to say,
I don't ask for much I am easily pleased,
But life on the road is no longer the way,
And I am finding it harder to get through each day.

There once was a time, when the open road,
Meant adventure, excitement, the chance to roam free,
But now there's no room for the vagrant's code,
And no one will invite you to tea, in this cold society.

I once had a friend who would tramp miles every day,
A constant companion, Bill Westway by name,
His knowledge and wit would make every one smile,
He was killed by some youths, whilst climbing a stile.

I've decided to hang up my boots, as it were,
And have managed to take up with a lady quite fair,
She appears to think of me quite nicely it seems,
But I am still on the road with old Bill, in my dreams.

May 8, 2014

An Exercise In Alliteration

The garrulous, Greek grape gatherers,
Joined joyously with jocund japes,
The olive pickers and ostrich pluckers,
Celebrating the season's success in song.

The querulous quiver of musical quavers,
From a quorum of quality wine quaffers
Reverberated robustly round the room,
And resonated rhythmically from the roof's rafters.

An altercation arose amongst some aggressive Athenians,
Averting an armed argument was avoided adroitly,
By brave, bold buskers, brusquely berating their bombast,
And loudly and laudably lamenting such loutish leanings.

Personally I drank my Retsina and went back to my Hotel.

May 8, 2014

Damian Cranney

Love's Tragedy

Sadness and sighing,
lie in bed together, crying,
There is no need to be upset,
He said; but softly,

I am here for you,
Please, let me stay,
Your fears I know,
Would go away.

For I will smooth your brow,
And comfort you,
I will be with you,
Until the day's new dawn.

And when you lie in slumber,
I will be there too,
My love will be a blanket,
And protection from the storm.

She turned and
looked at him with sadness,
The hurt inside,
Would never wane.

The Waterfall of Life

To forgive him,
Would be nought but madness,
But how else,
Could she ease the pain?

It is too late, she said,
The time has passed,
My trust in you is dead,
My hopes dashed.

She had found him in the arms,
Of her closest friend,
The bond was broken,
Love's tragedy, its end.

May 8, 2014

Love's Rejuvenation

Procrastination steals the time,
that lovers could use better,
Forgiveness is not easy,
but if not released will fester.

Regrets live on, when love is gone,
unless rejuvenated,
Time passes and will heal the hurt,
'Love's tragedy' created.

And so it was two lives re-crossed,
fate defined their future,
The hurt had passed; they now could laugh,
each with the other.

What had seemed a grievous act,
which never forgot could be,
Was frivolous and petty,
now their love had been set free.

For friends of these two loves,
The break had been traumatic,
Some had taken sides,
And so the healing was sporadic.

The Waterfall of Life

Like a pebble causing ripples,
we affect all those we care for,
However love is blind,
and takes no mind if others hurt more.

May 8, 2014

Damian Cranney

The Wife

She sat across the room in deep concentration,
Watching Tv with avid fascination,
She is as desirable now as the day we first met,
We've had our differences, but never had regret.

She has a fiery temper, that really is quite cute,
But blind love, no faults does see and so keeps mute,
We have been together now, for a very long time,
This crotchety, slightly deaf, lovely little lady of mine.

We are not yet in our dotage I am happy to say,
And my passion for her grows more each and every day,
But life bound together as lovers and friends,
Makes you understand more, that love never ends.

Having said all of that, l will have to admit,
That I get on her nerves, I'm afraid, quite a bit,
None of us are perfect, in my case not at all,
And if I argue that perfection is all about perception,
I know that ground is rocky and I'm heading for a fall.

We sometimes bicker all day long in happy procrastination,
And disagree on everything that happens in our nation,
This does not detract from how we feel about the other,
I sometimes think her wrong, but do not care, 'cos I love her.

May 8, 2014

The Soul's Passage

I was there at the dawn of time,
When life began I was in my prime,
Observed the big bang which created it,
And, was there when the first amoeba split.

I shared my soul, and have always been with you,
As you grew, so my souls grew too,
The life force is for all, not just a few,
The last will be first, for no one is passed over.

But I will be with you, as long as you're with me,
For I am the reincarnation of all that you see,
Each and every all of us have been here before,
And we all will be present at the final judgement door.

May 8, 2014

Damian Cranney

Prescribed Poetry

When poetry is deftly penned,
It has the power to briefly lend,
A key to open up extant,
Emotions that lie dormant.

Our daily lives are strewn with stress,
Our feelings, deep inside, repressed,
A moment's pause, to briefly read,
Another's thoughts can relieve the need.

Death is the ultimate rest,
But avoiding that deep slumber's, best,
Peace of mind, and remaining calm,
Are helped by poetry's proven charm.

The next time, life to you seems sad,
And everything you do turns bad,
Pick up a tome of proven worth,
And it will salve your mood's low dearth.

May 8, 2014

Death

Vaunted death thy powers are great,

You wield them against both vale and state,

No one is safe once within your arms,

Great or small they succumb to your charms.

But hold, before you bloat with pride,

For, you are only a vehicle, to the other side,

So do not gloat, or think you're higher,

You serve us merely as a taxi for hire.

Without you we could not rise to glory,

To join the Lord and laugh at Hell's fury,

So death, your services we will no longer require,

Go take yourself off; it is your turn to expire.

May 8, 2014

Dangerous Seas

On a night much like tonight, and as I stood outside my door,
I heard some sounds that set me tingling,
Much like distant church bells ringing,
A peel for help, was in their clarion,
Ringing round from heath to town, above the ocean roar,
All who lived in this small hamlet knew that sound from yore,
It was a knell that would be sounded,
Just before a boat was grounded,
Grounded on the rocky coastline, or the rocky shore,
Signifying danger, it was a sound you can't ignore.

Next I saw Dan Glover running, to the lifeboat he was manning,
Then his Bosun, John, came through,
Followed by the lifeboats' crew,
All in eager expectation of helping those in dire distress,
Sailing out in any weather, braving sea, and night's darkness.

It was many hours later, that these brave lads came ashore,
They had rescued three poor seamen, from a crew of four,
Yet again they'd faced that maelstrom,
All that nature's wildness came from,
Had faced it and had won, against the odds, and nature's law.

May 8, 2014

Let The Earth Breathe

The lungs of earth, are being attacked,
If we want to keep breathing it's now we should act,
If not for the sake of our own peace of mind,
Then for our children's children and all of mankind.

Trees by themselves are a beautiful sight,
Aesthetically pleasing in their own right,
But of greater importance and why we should care,
The trees and the plankton, provide all of our air.

A forest the size of a small country, I fear,
Is torn, from the face of our planet each year,
To anthropomorphise the earth as a metaphor,
From space you would see it trying to breathe more.

There are many things that require our attention,
But gasping for breath is one we should mention,
Please all plant a tree, well more if you can,
To be more eco-friendly sounds like a plan.

May 8, 2014

Damian Cranney

Go Fishing

There is no peace to equal that,
of fishing by a lake,
or a stream, or river broad,
or pond within a wood.

If worries you would cast away,
Take a fishing break,
Nature, is the balm that soothes,
The restless soul for good.

I remember, one idyllic,
sunny day in spring,
Rising early, well before,
Dawn's tentative groping light.

Arriving at the lake to hear,
a far-off robin sing,
A ripple from a rising fish,
all added to the sight.

To angle for your supper,
Is reward enough, it's true,
But that day, was a record day,
eleven trout all told.

The Waterfall of Life

It fed the family well,
perhaps a week or two,
But memories of that treasured day,
is what inside, we hold.

However if excitement,
is what you're craving for,
Fishing in a little boat,
upon a rolling sea.

Buffeted by waves and wind,
not too far from the shore,
Satisfies the need inside
and makes our souls run free.

Fighting fish and nature,
whatever form, you choose,
Fresh water or the salty brine,
The outcome is the same.

Catching cod and mackerel,
you later have for tea,
Is wonderful, I promise you,
And part of life's rich game.

May 10, 2014

Damian Cranney

Life's Road

When in my youth I knew the truth,
To all of life's stark questions,
With flippant ease, to please or tease,
I had the answer, could seize the day,
Was sure of myself, in every way.

When in the middle years of life,
I matured a bit, could take advice,
The world, was still all mine to conquer,
But it didn't matter now, if it took a little longer,
Diverted by indulgence, in the luxuries of life,
Whilst coping with the problems, of daily toil and strife.

Now comes the rub, time ticks its knell
Good intentions, will pave our own road to hell,
And all those things that we thought could wait,
Chances are that we probably, have left it too late,
You can change it of course, it depends on how well,
You react to this warning, only you can tell.

So let us stop tempting, the arbiters of fate,
Grasp life by the throat, and not hesitate,
We have it within us, to map our own course,
The route may have to be taken with force,
But obstacles are only problems not solved,
Just meet them head on until all is resolved.

May 10, 2014

You Are My Love

You are my love, needs I say more,
Must I with, fancy words to state,
expound upon my need for you,
And with a lovesick phrase relate,
That without you, life's such a bore,
And that I need you more and more.

Yes, needs I must, for it is true?
You are all to me, without; within,
To feed my insatiable lover's whims,
Wrapped within mine heart are you,
My world is you, I need no other view.

Delicate Love, flying on gossamer wings,
Loves that have gone before, cast shadows,
But having gone are but ephemeral things,
Forget the past, this love now, is not like those,
And out of all that may have been, it is you I chose.

May 10, 2014

Can I Buy Some Happiness Please?

I am grateful for having been granted,
This life, such as it may be,
The simplest of things still make me enchanted,
But I know there's much more, than the little I see.

A new born child grips your finger, with tiny baby hands,
And later when it smiles, and shows it understands,
That you will always be there, no matter what befalls,
And the child becomes Adult, it's that moment one recalls.

Life is made up of moments like these,
So is there a price you must pay for it please?
You have to give, before you can take,
And it's yourself that you give, and for your own sake.

The sum of all happiness, is human interaction,
But the only way it works is if it's selfless benefaction,
If aims are materialistic your rewards you will receive,
But happiness it will not buy, do not yourself, deceive.

May 12, 2014

Date With A Vampire

There once was a vampire quite fat,
Who was partial to fricassee of rat?
He liked to drink blood, but rat he did favour,
It really was quite peculiar behaviour.

But Vladimir had more problems than that,
He no longer could turn himself into a bat,
He still had the need to hang upside down,
So would stand on his head, in a dressing gown.

He went on a date with a zombie, of late,
Who though recently deceased, he really did rate,
It was going quite well, till they got up to dance,
When, Zelda the Zombie went into a trance.

She was still for a moment but started to shake,
And then parts of her body began to break,
Her arms fell off first and then her head,
But the loss of her legs stopped the evening dead.

Vladimir kept his composure quite well,
He was disappointed of course but you couldn't tell,
He picked her up gently, and sent her home in a cab,
He has a date with her next week, at Frankfurters' Lab.

May 14, 2014

Damian Cranney

Lying Not Standing

I knew she was lying,
when I saw her still in bed,
When she's not lying, but standing,
She nearly reaches my head.

But being horizontal,
She barely comes up to my knees,
And that goes for everyone,
In varying degrees.

Of course there are those,
Who practise lying for a living,
Politicians, when speaking,
You know, will not be giving.

Any of the things, they promise,
In their bloated speeches,
And nothing they do, that's good,
Is ever going to reach us.

How can you tell,
Someone is acting mendacious?
Their body tells the truth,
They start by being loquacious.

The Waterfall of Life

Their eyes start to wander,
Ever so slightly,
They gesticulate wildly,
And grasp their hands tightly,
To avoid being hurt,
You'll have to move more sprightly,
Do not procrastinate,
It will make you seem, unsightly.

But lying is part of the
Human condition,
There are white lies, slight lies,
and vague supposition.

But the ones that hurt the most,
Are those that deceive,
Destroying your faith and trust,
In who you can, believe.

Remember the salesman's art,
If trust you would engender,
Sincerity is the major key,
If belief you want to render.

Whatever ploy he uses,
Being sincere,

Damian Cranney

Will leave it in the shade,
'Cos once he can fake sincerity,
You know he's got it made!

The last verse, obviously,
Was being quite facetious,
No one would advocate,
Being that devious.

But some organisations,
Encourage staff to say,
Anything, that culminates in,
A sale for them that day.

The moral of this verse is,
Whatever you do, be truthful,
Although when it comes to people,
I'm cynical and rueful.

You have to make a stand,
in this world of dissimulation,
To fabricate with good intent
Lessens, not your participation.

May 24, 2014

Forgive You Your Sins

Go, save yourself from sinning,
The end is almost nigh,
But then again why bother?
The world is full of sin,
And your trivial contribution,
Will not impact at all,
'Cos relative to the real bad guys,
Your badness is quite small.

Your nasty thoughts and petty lies,
Make you feel your evil,
A state of mind, inherited,
From times quite medieval,
The bad amongst us sold their souls,
And they make you look angelic,
They place into perspective,
Your actions and your malice,
Do not allow self-hate to rule,
It will only make you callous.

June 6, 2014

Damian Cranney

An Independent Scotland (Or, Beware The English)

An independent Scotland,
That will do just fine,
We no longer have to listen,
To the Scots' familiar line,
Whatever woe that land has had,
Is laid at England's door,
But if you analyse the truth,
We're being blamed, what for?

More Scotsmen have been killed by Scots,
That's no lie,
William Wallace, his history,
Perverted by Gibson, did die,
Betrayed by the Bruce,
Who took the crown at Scone,
After killing, John Comyn,
Who had the right to the throne.

What about, the bonnie brave lads,
Abandoned at Culloden?
With empty bellies, and broken hearts,
Their prince they saw depart.
A third of those they faced were Scots,

The Waterfall of Life

Some Irish and some German,
Cumberland, commanded,
Officers were usually called, Campbell or Urquart.

Clan rivalry has a lot to answer,
Especially at Glencoe,
The Campbells and Macdonalds,
Considered each a foe,
But Macdonald was polite to guests,
Who'd disturbed him from his bed,
With instructions to arrest him,
The Campbells killed them all instead.

The clearances took place,
Run by, local Scottish factors,
Employed by landlords who were Scots,
Not English detractors,
The worst one of all,
Was a lawyer born in Moray,
Patrick Sellar, was his name,
And it's Scotland he put to shame.

Scotland was a barren place,
For crofters of that stoic race,
That is why they fled the land,
And yes it was a big disgrace,

But if the bleak and wild terrain,
Proved hard their families to maintain,
Why is an Englishman to blame,
When foreign soil can't life sustain?

Before we joined together,
In unhappy unity,
Our security was always threatened,
By our old north enemy,
Whoever hated England,
Found a friend and ally there,
The answer was the union,
In which we both can share.

Make no mistake security,
Was why we joined together,
If Scotland is a foreign state,
It could be viewed as an open gate,
The natural progression will be,
Border controls for you and me,
On a personal note I'll stop the scotch,
My favour will be, for Irish whiskey.

June 15, 2014

Two Lives Together

A tender touch upon your face,
A gentle caress while in bed you lie,
An arm, around you, in loving embrace,
And she in languorous repose gives out a sigh.

You have the day ahead to share,
The adventure is about to start anew,
She is my world of that I am aware,
I lay my soul quite bare to state that view.

You linger over breakfast; her gaze has you enthralled,
It is caught forever in the camera of your mind,
That moment lives within you to always be recalled,
And the years will polish it and make it more defined.

You reach the age when the life you've spent together,
Is longer than the time before you met,
You know you want to be with her forever,
And all the things you've shared you never will forget.

July 17, 2014

Don't Vacillate

Let not adversity, douse the fire within,
Or undue critics deviate your way,
Your being has a natural propensity to win,
Challenge life, don't vacillate or sway.

Question the wrath of those who see no merit,
In simple pleasures the soul enjoys to play,
Bounteous nature our legacy to inherit,
Needs our protection, if we are to enjoy each day.

Revel in the uniqueness of yourself, rejoice,
Forgetting not you walk this path but once,
The course is set, make wise your choice,
And never listen to that negative inner voice.

July 18, 2014

The Tallyman Of Life

Age, will not render her less to me,
The memories like fruit are palpable and ripe,
The inner eye unravels all we see,
Separating the real from what is merely hype.

Death or fear of death when years have passed,
No longer haunt, like it did in youth,
But living death when memory is gone and past,
A stranger to all she loves, is what she dreads in truth.

Her father, as affable as any man I've known,
Suffered from this malady of advancing senility,
Gradually, almost imperceptibly into a child he'd grown,
The helplessness you feel, reveals your own stark inability.

Do not yourself condemn, just be there,
It's all part of the better or the worse,
That you promised you would share,
The tallyman is knocking just open up your purse.

August 7, 2014

A Life In Shadow

I cannot bear to see you there,
Upon that chair in solitary recline.
It seems not fair, that I cannot share,
your company, for which I pine.

Although the shell that is and was you,
Appears to be on open view,
The you that previously was us, is gone,
Lost like the sun, that once upon us shone.

As we fade into the darkness, of infinite night,
lost amongst the shadow, perhaps bereft of light.
I will always be there, showing you the way,
If there's a light I'll find it, time is relative, they say.

This was a dream from which I woke
Reflecting fears that might soon be,
That nether world where sleep holds sway,
Sometimes shows truths, hidden by the light of day.

September 13, 2014

We Hope You Stay But If You Go

Impassioned pleas seem not of merit,
When un-conjoined with sincere grace,
Scotland will always have its culture to inherit,
Joined with Britain, in brotherhood and race.

Do not go into the darkness,
Without at least some taper light,
Boldness makes you brave and fearless,
But is not a shield, when you have to fight.

Let us march together,
Away from the dark unknown,
Strength in unison is safer,
Unless you're in the tomb,
Let not those, who would divide us,
Win, when the race is almost won.

People split by nationalist fervour,
Foment the hate, of racial pride,
That is a darker place to vote for,
Don't end up on the devil's side.

What if you do? We'll wave goodbye,
Not in anger, but in sorrow,
And once you're gone, I will not lie,
We will carry on into a new tomorrow,
With the freedom our own path to follow.

September 13, 2014

In Between The Light And Dark

In between the light and dark,
When thoughts roam free unhindered,
When solitary contemplation reaps,
Its own reward before one sleeps.

The treasures of the mind enclosed,
In stasis, locked by our own fears,
In reverie, released and unencumbered,
A creative spark not seen, that slumbered.

To open up the mind, and give it rein to wander,
To freely follow paths that once you would not enter,
Should be your aim and resolute pursuit,
If you lose your way, no matter, there's always another route.

July 4, 2015

Damian Cranney

Cast Off Your Shrouds

I want to be shaded, from the weather's blight,
Protected from the wind and lightning's flight,
I want to be lodged and screened from the sea,
Blanketed by an azure sky, within the valley's lea.

And having wandered to this place,
I don't want to hustle, I don't want to chase,
My only desire is just to be,
Left in thoughtful reverie.

There are days like these, when life seems dim,
Your pot has been filled. But not to the brim,
You can like it or lump it, no change will ensue,
But at least to yourself you can always be true.

Give me a starry night, unfilled with clouds,
Uplift your spirits, cast off the shrouds.
Gaze in wonder, at this awe-inspiring sight,
But know those distant suns are dead,
Despite their look so bright.

And so it is with the human condition,
We all look bright despite our perdition,
We shuffle along in a queue to the grave,
Hoping that light, (that's our soul) we will save.

September 14, 2015

Wide Sad Eyes

A little child with wide sad eyes,
Looked straight at me, as I watched TV,
A migrant, a refugee, it took me by surprise,
Because, a child in distress was all I could see.

Her Father held her in protective embrace,
Pleading for help, tears covering his face,
They should not be labelled, no judgement made,
All we should do is just come to their aid.

Will the world never learn, that war will not stop?
The warlords who draw swords, and kill for the sake,
Perhaps they all should be burnt at the stake,
But that makes us just as bad, to my mind,
Because they are still all, part of mankind.

September 19, 2015

Damian Cranney

In Memory Of

Everyone is remembered by someone,
For two generations they say,
How long is the memory for those who have gone,
Before all that they were, has just faded away?

If you're famous for being notorious,
Or a general for being victorious,
History will have a note we can find,
And you always will be in the public mind.

To the man in the street, that does not matter,
As long as he's included in his family's chatter,
And his characteristics are passed on to his kin,
Means he's always remembered by them from within.

September 20, 2015

The Crack

The emaciated body,

Looking like a resident from Dachau,

Sat on the park bench,

Staring vacantly with soulless eyes.

A once vibrant and beautiful child,

Adored by her family and friends,

Reduced down to a sale of herself, for some ale,

Or a fix from some pricks who played free with their dicks,

Who would sell her some crack,

And did not care for the fact,

That her life would remain, forever in chains.

They are part of the filth, that society spawns,

They are allowed to survive and to deal and to jive,

They will always be there 'cos we really don't care,

As long as they stay, somewhere else while we play,

It is not until when,

one of yours starts to change,

And you know something's wrong,

Because they are acting so strange,

The bastards now have them,

they will never let go,
So you now start to question,
To shout and to yell,
I'm afraid that you've probably left it too late,
For her parents did that, and they still live in hell.

March 22, 2016

A Pebbled Beach

I walked along a pebbled beach,
and gazed far out to the ocean's reach,
Surrounded by the sounds of surf,
And soaring seagulls squawking.

The ocean met the darkening sky,
As voluminous black clouds on high,
Joined with a burgeoning storm below,
That made the waves crash noisily,
As they beat against the shore.

It was a mighty and majestic sight,
As evening's approach banished the light,
It was with regret, that an exit was made,
To a warm welcome cafe, serving tea and cake,
I would also commend the strawberry shake.

We returned next day to a calm flat sea,
The pebbles were wet and reflected the sun,
Sparkling like jewels with a background of blue,
And multifarious colours, each with a different hue.

March 24, 2016

Damian Cranney

A Vote For Freedom

With joined endeavour our country will endure,
The world was shaped by what we did and saw,
We may in izzard fashion flags have planted,
And left native feathers ruffled but enchanted,
It's reason why their children to our shores do flock,
They dream to be here but our ways they mock.

All cultures here have always found a place,
To settle and amalgamate their race,
A multi-cultural melting pot of hope,
Whose numbers now we find hard to cope,
The hopes and fears of all this hapless mass,
Cannot be solved by giving all a pass,
Ten million souls are clamouring at our door,
We have no room to take in any more.

But let us give them and ourselves an aim,
Let's take control and vote to not remain,
By leaving we have everything to gain,
Have courage to take charge of our own fate,
Now is the time, the future is too late,
The 23rd of June is not a day, it is a date,
Be there, do not share, make us self-aware.

June 13, 2016

Independence Day

A Great Day For Freedom

The 23rd of June 2016,
A noble day, a great day,
The day the people had their say,
But if Remainers had won the vote,
They would pontificate and preen,
That democracy in action had been seen,
and boast of principles not compromised.
That their democratic ideals were realised,
Would be incensed if you questioned their win,
Yet are happy for self-interest to indulge in that sin.

The Remainers all want to overturn,
The principles we all must learn,
The values that define a nation,
Should not be lightly cast aside,
Do none of them have any pride?
The vote is made, the die is cast,
Do not ignore our noble past.

Remainers, this was not your turn,
you know you've got it wrong,
One day this tragic treachery,
will be refrained in song.

Damian Cranney

Democracy nearly died today,
you tried to killed it with your lies,
The majority who voted 'yes'
Ignored you and gave full redress,
Ensuring freedom for us all,
With hope, we now, can all walk tall.

The little man, he had his day
but then you shot him down,
Ecstatic when he won the fray.
He little knew that you would say,
We do not think you know enough,
besides you look a little rough.
I stand to lose my job,
and probably all my money,
I think it's best if you don't count,
and then my future's sunny.

Don't worry, we'll look after you,
providing there's no fuss,
We'll have to change some rules of course,
so this again, won't happen,
Give it a year or two,
I doubt that you'll remember,
And going to the polls to vote,
will be a cold dead ember.

To Remain where we don't have to think,
Where absent honour hides its face,
The race fair won, to you means nought.

Where is your conscience, your shame to trace?
Your fairness, of which you give no thought,
Our values are by you demeaned,
Our most loved Land that you disgrace,
If the referendum is overturned, then Democracy is dead.
RIP

June 28, 2016

Damian Cranney

A Place Without A View

Do not let those who are jealous or mean,
Make you unhappy by creating a scene,
Just because they have a bad disposition,
Shouldn't make you their natural opposition.

Just lately the world has taken off in directions,
that are not that conducive to our health or digestions,
Everyone seems to be unsure or uncertain,
Their future seems hidden behind a dark curtain.

Perhaps they are victims of mass paranoia,
But terrorists abound and are all very real,
So the dangers seem vast but also surreal,
The turmoil is global but the causes aren't noble.

I long for the time when if you wanted you could,
Just take yourself off and get lost in a wood,
And it would not matter which path you take,
'Cos you probably would find yourself next to a lake.

The problem we have today you will find,
Is information overload that disturbs our mind,
It would be great if we could just turn off the news,
And not be aware, and yes not have any views!

July 29, 2016

A Chance Encounter

That winsome look upon her face,
Her coy manner when in love's embrace,
The memories of a knowing smile,
That linger and haunt me for a while.

I knew her once upon a time,
A fairy story set to rhyme,
I never have forgotten her,
She was so vibrant and, so fair,

And it was just by Chance, today,
When shopping in the usual way,
I came upon a vision bright,
Of her, bathed in bright sunlight.

She stood there smiling back at me,
And suddenly we both could see,
That fate had played a part somehow,
In shaping past and future, into now.

August 2, 2016

Damian Cranney

Nature's Design

I walked by a winding babbling brook,
Which reflected like stars the beams of the sun,
As they shone on the watery stream having fun,
And the ground was all dappled, in shadow and light,
Creating a picture of contrasting delight.

The day was just meant to be enjoyed to the full,
As a warm balmy wind rustled leaves in the trees,
And a carpet of bluebells were surrounded by bees,
I followed the path that others had worn,
Past a field with some lambs recently shorn.

I was worried because of a fox I had seen,
And as if to confirm my worst fears had been right,
I came upon a sheep, hurt in a fight,
I tried to get near, but its fear made that risky,
However, it was still alive and frisky.

The rest of the day was spent wandering and free,
And for a short while I rested, under a tree,
At the edge of the woods, with the sun in decline,
I made my way home in a mood quite benign,
Thinking how wonderful is nature's design.

August 3, 2016

The Babs Of Koth

Do not go down to the Bullymoth,
Where the Dammberat is King,
For he cares not for us Babs of Koth,
He will flabber you with his baddering,
And then bind you with gullottal string.

His power stems from the ring of Doom,
Which he stole from the Goblin Lord,
It was forged on the mystic Hagar loom,
by the mighty Hobs of Mord.

I plead again with you my son,
Keep away from that hateful monarch,
Leave behind your sword of megatron,
And go not into the woods of dark.

No one has returned from out that place,
Where the Jamberdrag destroys without trace,
And roars till the very earth does shake,
And then flies off to his sylvan lake.
I plead again, do not, do not, do not,
Go down to the Bullymoth.

Damian Cranney

I take your point his son replied,
But where would that leave me in my pride,
How could I hold my head up high,
If all the girls of Koth, would sigh,
Unable to look me in the eye.

His father sighed and shook his head,
And his son picked up his sword,
He marched off to the woods of dark,
And down to the Bullymoth.
He's not been seen or heard of since,
Perhaps he lives or perhaps he's dead,
But no more Babs of Koth,
Go down to the Bullymoth.

August 7, 2016

The Man In The Dock

Judge Mayer on the bench did sit,
Coldly appraising the man in the dock,
The man in the dock was unperturbed,
He gave the judge a knowing wink,
At least that's what the judge did think,
For which he was not at all prepared, and it gave him quite a shock.

"Now, now, my man we'll have none of that,"
and then he noticed he was wearing a hat.
"You cannot wear that hat in court,
take it off right now I know your sort."
The man stayed cool as cool can be,
"I'm sorry M'Lord, I cannot comply,
I have to wear it and that's no lie."

"You have to wear it, don't be absurd,
That's the stupidest thing I've ever heard."
"It's true M'Lud," the man decried,
"Let me explain and then you decide,
It's part of my job, I'm a beekeeper by trade,
It's how I keep them all warm when I go on Parade."

"I've never heard anything so ridiculous as that,
people don't keep bees living in their hat,
If you don't take it off the sergeant will remove it."
"Alright," said the man, "if you really insist."
And he ripped his hat off with a twist of the wrist.

Suddenly the room was filled, with a swarm full of bees,
and everyone there just dropped to their knees,
"Clear the court," said the judge to the sergeant at arms,
As in panic he turned on all the alarms,
And ran into his chambers, locking the door,
No one was left but the man in the dock,
And as he walked out the door of the court,
He turned to a friend waiting under the clock,
Works every time with that judge's sort!

August 8, 2016

Bubble The Rat

Bubble the rat knew all of the words,
Of all the songs that you've ever heard,
He would sing in church below the nave,
And would accompany grieving mourners,
As they all stood round the grave.

He also liked singing at the local school,
But was not allowed in as general rule,
The head you see did not like Bubble,
Rats he said, were nothing but trouble.

Bubbles decided to go semi Pro,
And got himself booked at a local show,
He did so well he was asked back again,
He's been really successful ever since then.

He occasionally sees prejudice against rats,
But that's nothing new some people don't like bats,
He always remains calm, and ignores the bigotry,
I just want to sing he says, and left to be free.

August 10, 2016

Damian Cranney

War Graves Visit

Across a dreadful field I walked,
Where bodies lay all torn and bent,
Their eyeless gaze stared back at me,
It seemed, I thought, accusingly.

I rushed out of the cemetery,
And looking back neat rows of graves,
Was all that I could see,
And all the souls that therein lie,
Were calm at rest under an azure sky.

I cannot conceive what happened there,
But what I saw in that brief time,
Was real to me, for they were there,
A cry of anguish, they wished to share?

In Flanders fields the rows of white,
Testify to that first great fight,
It was the war to end all wars,
But the killing won't stop, whatever the cause.

August 22, 2016

The Orb

I awoke from a sleep,
In the middle of the night,
In need of a nice cup of tea,
A refreshing brew,
Would put me just right,
From a restless sleep,
It would set me free.

Pottering in the kitchen,
Waiting for the kettle,
I felt the hairs on my neck,
Begin to rise,
And a palpable coldness,
That around me did settle.

Fear and fascination,
Left me frozen me in surprise.

Suddenly a bright orb appeared,
Floating in mid-air,
Mesmerised I watched it,
Travel around the room.
And as it did another joined it,
Over by the broom.

October 11, 2016

The Powers That Be

Effectively, the powers that be,
Were rocked in their tower, by a plebian sea,
Shaken to the core by just ordinary folk,
They belittle the result, as a very poor joke,
We must not let them douse the light,
And cast us all back into the night.

Not since the Athenians stood side by side,
Has Democracy in action, been seen and applied,
The biggest democratic move, by a nation,
has just taken place and has caused a sensation,
The people walked, no need to run,
they knew instinctively what had to be done.

But the hidden agenda of the Ruling elite,
Using guile and deceit, their aims to complete,
Is to kill the will of our proud nation race,
What they are trying to do is a total disgrace,
Platitudes and attitudes are all that remain,
Non-implementation obviously their aim.

The Waterfall of Life

The people's reaction will be more than distraction,
They will waken a fire and the country's dire ire,
If they thwart any more, the justified score,
If a football team loses when the others scored more,
You can't change the outcome by dissimulation,
Yet they happily ignore, the will of the nation.

November 17, 2016

Damian Cranney

Scotland Be Brave

Scotland oh! Scotland,
What have we done to thee,
That thou should'st want to part
When brothers both are we?

Have we not fought for freedom's sake,
side by bloody side?
And have we not shed both our blood,
in mutual victorious pride?
What do we say, to those who laid,
their lives down for our future,
Do we not owe it to the past,
to keep the bonds that bind us fast?

Should we not celebrate,
The differences that make us great,
And that together, unity,
is both our destiny and fate?

Would the square at Waterloo have held,
IIf tartan had been absent,
If the fife and drums, in solitary refrain,
had no' the pipes to vent?

The Waterfall of Life

Would Sevastopol still hold the walls,
and would we be outside them?
We've been over the top, under the wire,
together we've suffered enemy fire.

The enemy now are those,
who have an interest in disunion,
"Divide and conquer", "fan the hate",
Let's hope to God it's not too late.

Let us have faith in common sense,
Stop balancing, on that unsafe fence,
Together we punch above our weight,
The union ensures, we will always be great.

We will forever be, a unique constitution,
Breaking with Europe is just restitution,
Staying conjoined in mutual respect,
With friendship and trust and time to reflect.

Do not let the wee lassie with evil intent,
Deviate the future, we now have been lent,
Do not let her vandalise, divert or destroy,
The gift of freedom that we now can deploy.

December 29, 2016

Spectral Dream

I found myself in a distant place,
An ethereal presence was by my side,
Surrounded by trees in a darkened wood,
I instinctively felt,
He was to be my guide.

To where, I dared not guess or know,
This chimera beckoned me to follow,
towards where I saw a light shine bright,
Down a craggy lane into a hollow.

The forest around me seemed alive,
As I followed the spirit towards the light,
The spectre stopped and pointed down,
Where my gaze fell on a piteous sight.

There before me all writhing in pain,
Were soldiers who fell on Flanders fields,
Towards the light they tried to crawl,
And those who got there rose into the air.

The scene dissipated and turned into mist,
That I should rise next I quickly dismissed,
Waking from a dream I breathed a big sigh,
At least not today would I rise into the sky.

January 14, 2017

The Ex-Soldier - An Allegory

A foul furtive fellow,
came a-knocking at Joe's door -
"What doth thou want,
Thou craven knave?
Speak up else I put thee in thy grave."

"I mean no harm my master,"
The ill looking creature moaned,
"I ask for but a bite of bread,"
and he turned away and groaned.

"A pox upon your body,
and a curse upon your soul,
Have I been put upon this earth,
to feed the likes of you?
A beggar and a vagrant,
and perhaps a cut throat too,
Be gone before I fetch my whip,
and tan your hide to blue."

The beggar looked at Joe,
and something in him stirred,
"Just now I called thee master,
But thou art nothing but a turd,
You treat me like a dog thou cur,

I will not leave your sullied path,
Until you call me sir."

Big Joe could not believe his ears,
and one step forward did he take,
The beggar now to action took,
His sprightly frame belied his look,
and from beneath his ragged cloak,
Pulled a heavy wooden stave of oak.

"I may, on hard times, have fallen,
Swallowed pride and not been outspoken,
T'was before my soul had been broken,
for I once was a soldier a good one to boot,
With crossbow I could any man outshoot,
Accoutred with short sword and pike,
I could hold my own with anyone you like."

Although not afraid Joe,
looked at him wry,
Perhaps his harsh words,
had been hasty,
He looked at him now,
with a new look in his eye,
"Wouldst like a taste,

of wife's new baked pie?
I am happy good sir,
to try thee at quarterstaff,
But prithee refresh thee,
with some pie and some ale,
And you can regale us,
with your soldierly tale."

The soldier looked up,
a new light, bathed his face,
"I thank thee master
for thy most kind words,
They show thee a gentleman,
full of fine grace,
I pray forgiveness, if I,
offence to you have given,
Your words inside made me cry,
By them was my temper driven,
I am now the me, that I used to be,
I accept your offer most gratefully."

February 2, 2017

Damian Cranney

A Scottish Moor

I traversed a craggy Scottish moor,
Where morning mists,
rolled o'er,
the soft undulating ground,
smelling of peat,
Gave way to a rocky path beneath my feet.

A screeching sound I heard,
from way up high,
I looked and saw,
two goshawks flying by,
Circling as if in altercation,
I could not tell if it was fighting or flirtation,
A scrambling noise ahead drew my attention,
to a flock of sheep who,
in frightened apprehension,
eyed me warily,
but it did not stop them eating,
I passed them by,
and left them to their bleating.

The Waterfall of Life

Scotland has a wild,
and wondrous landscape,
Where unspoilt nature,
invites you to escape,
From rocky heights, to climb,
To which you would aspire,
To green encumbered glens,
that do inspire.

It grasps your soul, this land,
with its bounteous beauty,
And reminds that to protect it,
is your duty,
I will admit to other loves, and causes,
Shakespeare's sceptred isle,
is my amour,
But Robbie Burns' homeland,
I as much adore.

February 16, 2017

Damian Cranney

The Knight With No Name

The giant Droog dragon, enveloped in flames,
the Castle protecting the Knight With No Name,
From the gates of Pelligor, the Knight had set forth,
To the very walls of Hades, he set his course,
the fairy princess, had given him a quest,
To kill the Droog Dragon, in his very own nest.

He travelled by day and all through the night,
Traversed the dark forests where the goblins had right,
Crossed the valley of death avoiding the trolls,
And killed the giant gatekeeper in charge of the tolls.

The Dragon was protected by hell's chosen vassal,
The knight new no fear, he charged out of the castle,
Whatever happened now, the bold Knight knew,
His honour and courage would see him through.

And so it was recorded, in the ancient lays,
Which told of golden, halcyon days,
Where chivalry and honour triumphed,
Where Knights on horse, could overcome,
The mightiest Dragons, in any kingdom.

The Waterfall of Life

The Dragon fought well, it was mighty and strong,
The fire it spewed forth, was a hundred yards long,
But the Knight with No Name, brushed it aside,
And pushed his sword to the hilt, into the Dragon's side.

Roaring in agony, the giant beast fled,
But trying to fly, to the ground it crashed, dead,
The anonymous Knight, with easy nonchalance,
Walked past the Dragon, not looking back once.

The roars from the castle, of joy and amaze,
He acknowledged with a single solitary wave,
And mounting his horse, with a jingling of spurs,
The Droog Dragon dead, and no longer a curse.

February 21, 2017

England

England, my England, is everything to me,
From the greenest of its pastures,
protected by the sea,
To good old London town,
Which will never let you down.

It's from here the lion roars,
Ever so loudly,
where you can walk,
in the footsteps of heroes, proudly.

From the people it has bred,
to the writers we have read,
With a constitution made by common law,
It's a living breathing entity created to ensure,
that our freedom and our rights are not usurped.

A land of common sense and decency,
Where people live in harmony,
Extending help, to one another,
whether stranger or brother,
Believing all have a right,
to a stupid point of view,
And would fight for that right,
in defence of you.

This country of ours, is a land of peace and grace,
England puts a smile, smack upon your face,
so if you add it all together,
and despite inclement weather,
there's no better place, your weary head to rest,
and why England to all of us,
is the greatest and the best.

February 26, 2017

Damian Cranney

The Rape Of Poor Greece

Hellenic Greece,

admired and respected,

The father of democracy,

but never really tested.

In its historical youth,

was always seeking the truth,

Its philosophers taught us,

the why and the what,

their mathematicians taught us the how.

their orators used logic,

to avoid obfuscation,

Their play-wrights the stage,

to inform the Greek nation.

The centuries rolled by,

and its moment in time,

passed by,

and turned into a political crime.

They joined a club of friendly traders,

not knowing that they, were

'Political raiders'.

The Waterfall of Life

With bankers and bureaucrats, in collusion,

And having given up their own constitution,
the land of Socrates and Homer would see,
A version of their own,
Greek tragedy.

Move over Aristophanes,
this farce just writes itself,
no need for your heart to bleed,
put it back on the shelf.

The drama is enacted,
the deed has taken place,
You couldn't make it up,
you wouldn't be believed,
But for decades now, four in fact,
we all have been deceived.

The hemlock is administered,
the country is in mourning,
The reason for this hiatus,
finally now, is dawning,

Damian Cranney

The only way is out and up,
Drink no more,
from this poisonous cup,
friendship for Greece is, Global.

Is everywhere found,
Let not the anonymous Oligarchs,
furtively working like ravenous sharks,
Rob you of your precious ground.

March 6, 2017

Hidden Evil

The evil is hidden in those who deceive, You cannot perceive it, and so you believe,

Their lies and deceptions are clever and planned,

They prey on the vulnerable throughout the land.

Is it not time? is the question we ask,

To take up the baton, and address the task,

The young and the elderly, innocent and weak,

Are the targets the ruthless, set out to seek.

Tolerence at zero, is the least we should accept,

Maximum punishment, that the guilty should expect,

À little old lady answering the door,

Should not be afraid, worried or unsure.

A child playing innocently alone in the street,

Should not be at risk, from a stranger they meet,

The same principle applies to all whom we cherish,

Their lives are too precious, to allow them to perish.

March 21, 2017

Damian Cranney

Friends In Your Life

Last night in pensive mood I sat,
pondering on my thoughts,
unthinking.
It came into my mind,
how nice it would be, to talk,
with all the friends that I have known,
both in the pub,
when drinking.
As well as those when on a walk,
you met by chance,
which into friendship then had grown,
and time its magic did enhance.
Distance does not matter,
You can always be in touch,
by phone,
There is no need to be alone.

Work colleagues, then came to mind,
good and bad, nice or mean,
all played a part in forming me,
into me.
I would like to thank,
the ones who were kind,
and those that were not, I really don't mind,

The Waterfall of Life

They all form the fabric,
Of who I am now.
I am quite content,
with that somehow,
No regrets with a life,
full of friends heaven sent,
a loving family around me,
that is how it should be.

And of course my best friend,
the diamond in my life,
the slightly deaf,
but very cute, darling little wife.

March 21, 2017

The Soul's Progress

I walk in the shadow of death,

I have neglected to care for my soul,

Creeping age, brings it close with each breath,

Faith is the breath for your soul to be whole.

But when faith, no longer is there

And you've treated your soul like a shadow,

When its spiritual needs, you've ignored without care,

Leaving no room, to include and to share.

To the promises of church and state,

I now no longer relate,

I cast no blame, I assign no wrong,

But I cannot find salvation,

in a choral hymn or song.

Doctrine and catechism, drummed in by rote,

Never ever would get my vote,

The promise of everlasting damnation,

The subtle procrastination,

Hell fire just left me cold,

threats just made me bold,

rules designed to avoid temptation,

Were eschewed, when recognised,

as misinformation.

The Waterfall of Life

The future is what it will be,
If agnostic you're somehow set free,
To find God in your own special way,
To look forward with hope to that day.

In the meantime just follow these rules,
Just live for the day,
Do your best on the way,
And leave the hereafter,
To fate and to laughter.

March 29, 2017

Damian Cranney

Duties Reward

Smoke wafted across the village,
The swack, swack, swack, sound,
Of a helicopter inbound,
was heard,
Grass and dust churned and curled,
As it landed,
Amidst the carnage caused,
By its crew now disbanded,
The horrors of war,
are but nightmares when they sleep,
the traumas they live with,
they always will keep.

Just then he awoke,
from this dream,
Being kicked by a cop
in an alley not clean,
Wake up, wake up,
you can't sleep here,
He remembered his dream,
and had no fear.

I can sleep where I like,
I'm an ex-army vet,
I fought for my country,

which I do not regret,
But for all of that suffering,
I'm still owed a debt.

He found himself bound,
As the cop read his rights,
Was held hard to the ground,
Then thrown in the back,
Of a sleek, black and white,
Was charged and locked up,
In a cell for the night.

The judge in the morning,
Was unsympathetic,
If you're an ex veteran,
You should go get a job,
You make us feel guilty,
When you sleep in the street,
It was not our fault,
that you died in that war,
You just haven't realised,
You should not be here,
Eventually you will realise,
And will then disappear.

Damian Cranney

Thirty days was his sentence,
He was marched and locked in the cells,
The arresting officer treated him ok,
Would you like some pie? he heard him say,
Well thanks, said the vet,
No probs, said the cop,
What's your name I forget,
It's Robbo I guess, said the vet,
Mine's easy, the cop said, it's Joe.

I guess it ain't fair,
what was said just out there,
The cop said, as he handed him pie,
That's life, said the vet,
It's what I've come to expect,
And as he munched the food,
In desultory mood,
He gave out a long sad sigh.

Again he was locked,
In a six by nine cell,
Was he pissed off, I guess so,
But then who can tell?
He served the month out,

The Waterfall of Life

He had done this before,
And the lock on the door,
Made him feel more secure.

The time passed by, quite easy,
To him it was free board and lodge,
He picked up his things,
His wallet and rings,
They were matching,
And Joe had to ask,
Hey Rob, are you married?
I was but she died,
She was pregnant,
and the foetus miscarried,
While I was fighting away,
I guess that was, a really bad day.

That's tough, Joe the cop said,
That's life said the vet,
It's a bitch from the moment you're born,
You know it's not right,
But you just have to fight,
The fight is what keeps you alive.

But sometimes I want to,
just not to respond to,
The shit we get thrown every day.
With that he just went,
Joe watched him walk out of the door,
Who was that? said the sergeant,
I am afraid I don't know,
I have never seen him before.

April 1, 2017

Snowdonia Walks

I have from craggy Tryfan
gazed,
precariously crossed Crib Goch,
to amaze,
straddled Adam and Eve,
I do not deceive.

Looked down from Snowdon,
through the mist and the haze,
Walked all the hills,
enjoying the scene,
the view is inspiring, but also, serene.

I remember one weary, but very happy day,
enjoying each step as we made our way,
warmed by the sun,
inspired by the sight,
the whole of nature conspired to delight.

At the end of a long trek,
a pub came in view,
We were easily cajoled
into taking a pew.

Damian Cranney

Inside through dimpled windows,
shone the sun,
Its beams through golden glasses,
filled with beer,
created an atmosphere of friendship and cheer.

It wasn't long before,
we were quaffing pints of ale,
Surrounded by some new friends,
recounting their own tale.

By now we were hungry,
and the landlord did us proud,
I had a Barnsley chop with roasties,
and some veg,
and for afters, some apple pie.
with custard on the edge.

April 20, 2017

Fickle Fate

Mary Marion Williams, is one of twenty-three,
rescued and surviving the North Atlantic sea,
Fate is a fickle friend, to have upon your side,
For if destiny is written, there's no need to have a guide.

Mary believed in fate, so had no fear at all,
when on that dreadful night, the steward gave a call,
"Abandon ship, we're sinking," he rapped outside her door,
Then suddenly, an explosion threw her to the floor.

She did in no way panic,
Just picked herself up and dressed,
Paused for a moment, to root inside her chest,
Retaining a small object, and leaving all the rest,
Making her way to the deck above, the ship began to list,
she was struggling up the gangway, when someone grabbed her wrist,
Do not worry ma'am, a voice above her cried,
I am not, she said, I know I'm safe, for fate is on my side.

She was helped to a lifeboat, by a member of the crew,
and looking round, she found she'd joined, the other twenty-two,
Fate took a hand again, for our lucky ladyship,
She was picked up the very next day, by a Royal navy ship,

Who just by chance or maybe fate,
Happened to be passing, upon that very date.

This poem is a work of imagination, any likeness to persons living or dead is purely coincidental.

April 21, 2017

Follow That Stream

The fresh mountain water,

cascaded with glee,

Splashing and dashing,

over rocks and debris,

Churning and turning,

in unseemly haste,

No time on its way to the sea,

would it waste.

I followed its journey as well as I could,

Until I was blocked,

by an impassable wood,

The trees were so close,

and the bracken so dense,

I tried to skirt round it,

but was stopped by a fence.

Having decided to set up camp,

Just for the night,

I had only just pitched,

when the day lost its light,

I made myself cosy, with a safely lit fire,

eating sizzling sausages,

before I had to retire.

Damian Cranney

I awoke in a tent,
from a warm lethargic sleep,
nature also wakened,
from a sleep just as deep,

Enchanted and surrounded by the birds,
and other calls,
The constant noise and gushing,
from the nearby waterfalls.

I had to travel back that night,
I wish I could have stayed,
North Wales, is the place,
where, I mostly roam,
And luckily it's not that far,
from my home.

Driving back, the waning sun,
painted the clouds,
and the mountain tops bright,
In hues and shades, of golden light,
which then turned to shadows,
in the approaching dark of night.

April 23, 2017

The End Of The Pier

The end of the Pier was shrouded in mist,
the shadows we cast were defining,
We plighted our troth, and then we kissed,
'Neath a full orbed moon that was shining.

We walked hand in hand to the end of the Pier,
The ghosts of our past re-awakened our fear,
We had to be strong, for ourselves and each other,
Whether we could, we were about to discover.

The mist started lifting and in the moonlight,
A blanket of bats had just taken flight,
then in a moment the bats were not there,
they had completely dissipated into thin air.

We worked on the Pier, in our distant past,
It was closed, since we had been there last,
Whitby, supposedly, was where the vampires landed,
But this old Pier received them, before it was abandoned.

As we approached the door, that led into the Pier,
From the frightened flight of bats, one still was here,
A sudden metamorphosis took place within the frame,
And a vampire stood before us, I knew him, and his name.

Damian Cranney

Vladimir, I said to him, I once fought by your side,
I am your nemesis and fate, from me you cannot hide,
For I am here, to stop your cheer, and the evil that is you,
He gave me quite an evil look, deciding what to do.

I shined my torch upon his face,
Remembering how we loved this place,
The fair was now in disrepair,
But seeing Vladimir, we did not care.

The place had always been such fun,
especially when blessed, by a warm summer sun,
Vladimir was an amusement, placed within the fair,
whose main role it was, to frighten and to scare.

The Pier had no power, so we could not turn him on,
But the memory of what happened, has certainly not gone,
To animate the mannequin, it required a coin to go,
Then Vladimir would start, his ghoulish vampire show.

He would give an evil cackling laugh,
that shred your nerves apart,
He certainly was quite frightening,
and not for the faint of heart.

The Waterfall of Life

I suppose it was a funny place for us to reminisce,
But when in love there are memories, you do not want to miss,
I think we now are over the need to see the Pier,
Generally, we remember it, over a glass of beer,
I suppose we might go back one day and have a laugh at Vlad,
Although the old Pier's crumbling, it's really rather sad.

April 26, 2017

Shield Of Truth

I am lost in the darkness,
Blind to the light,
Struggling to find my way,
in this stygian night.

I know that there is somewhere,
A place prepared for me,
But my wanderings,
have not revealed,
What my destiny will be.

The world is spinning freely,
There is no one at the helm,
Gyrating wildly like a top,
Into a darker realm.

Send someone to guide me,
Is heaven that far away?
Where is my guardian angel,
To teach me how to pray.

If there is a God? then show me,
Let me see his face,
Give me understanding,
Help me moderate my pace.

The Waterfall of Life

I saw the sun this morning
It warmed my heart to see,
A new day now was dawning.
With the freedom to be free.

Truth is all that matters,
In that you must not yield,
Keep it always by your side,
And it will be your shield.

To Fly Like Birds

As if in a dream I hovered in flight,
The feeling was natural and a total delight,
I flew over fields, both fallow and green,
The cotton wool clouds, were part of the scene.

I landed with care, on a rocky hilltop,
The glider I hung from, did almost not stop,
Surveying the view with an appreciative eye,
Beneath billowing clouds in a pastel blue sky.

It was time to return, I looked over the edge,
And with great trepidation, launched off the ledge,
A thermal was rising, as I hurled off the hill,
It whirled me much higher, in an exhilarating thrill.

Man always has envied, the birds in the sky,
Wanting to emulate their ability to fly,
Hang gliding is the nearest to flying like birds,
But requires courage, as well as strong nerves.

May 4, 2017

Reasons For Drinking

The following four lines inspired my own poem, 'Reasons for Drinking'.

If you look it up on the web, it is described as an "anonymous Irish toast".

There are many good reasons for drinking,
And one has just entered my head,
If you can't have a drink when you're living,
How the hell can you drink when you're dead?

Reasons for drinking, there are quite a few,
some people might take a different point of view,
But if when alive, you abstain, I suggest,
That drinking when dead, is unlikely at best.

For those of us, who like to drink,
There is no harm in moderation,
A glass of wine is nice I think,
And aids contentment in our nation.

A philosopher, who only drank water,
condemned out of hand the demon drink,
He lectured both, his son and daughter,
On the dangers of drinking, gin that was pink.

Damian Cranney

My father once said, after quaffing a pint,
misquoting Marx, with impish delight,
That work was the curse of the drinking classes,
Then ordered a refill for all of our glasses.

Descartes had the answer, if we think, then we are,
He drew his inspiration, from a pickled gherkin jar,
He also liked to drink, a glass of vin de local,
Noticing that wine and veg, were, never ever vocal.

June 7, 2017

Love's Lost Time

A thunderous rumbling,
lightning flashing,
all within my troubled brain.
I wander in a daze,
afraid of crashing,
The cause is plain,
I must see you again.

The passing years,
where each does live,
In joy and sorrow,
and happiness spent.

Each with another,
who of themselves did give,
repaid by our lost time,
we to them lent.

It is not with covetous envy,
but with joy,
I look upon the sacrifice we made,
though self-interest now,
is what we must employ,
For what has gone before,
was but a masquerade.

Damian Cranney

Millennia come and go,
and decades fade away,
I know that we,
should not have parted,
And rue what happened,
on that fateful day,
But time will not give back,
what man has started.

Exacerbate the problem,
convolute the time,
Pick the optimum moment,
grab it if you can,
To love beyond reason,
is said to be no crime.
Insipid love, however,
has no passion or elan.
And wastes the little, that there is,
Of the time of man.

June 15, 2017

Who Cares! Have A Beer

These are the days of uncertainty
When all your beliefs are in question,
It engenders a state of melancholy,
Where the negatives get more attention.

The world is in flux, the turmoil is great,
All parties to life in a polarised state,
And if we must fight for our right to be here,
It is death and destruction, that we face, I fear,
Ahh! **** it, let's just have another pint of beer.

June 23, 2017

Damian Cranney

They Had No Choice

Go chase them from their dugouts,
Go chase them from their trench,
bayonet all their look outs,
ignore their dead's foul stench.

Tomorrow you go over,
The top, that is my lads,
and there is very little chance,
of your return from France.

The rattle of machine guns,
displace a man with space,
That space, is soon refilled,
with another of his race.

'No man's land,' is where they die,
their bodies all strewn around like chaff,
with eyes unblinking, to the sky,
Never again to smile or laugh.

This was the war, to end all wars,
Well that hope now lies buried,
Man cannot close hell's gaping doors,
his hope of peace, a losing cause.

The Waterfall of Life

It is not the dead that answer,
When you ask the question 'why',
But they showed us by example,
How to live and how to die.

Their lives they gave, for freedom's sake,
To save our heritage, their dream.
To remember them all, is the pledge we make,
Our debt their sacrifice, to redeem.

July 11, 2017

The Lie – Or Is It Alright To Tell A Little White Lie?

If someone is hurt,
By the truth you reveal,
Were the wounds engendered,
Will take time to heal.

Might it be better,
To spin a white lie,
To spare them from blushing,
And heaving a sigh?

Or perhaps you revel,
In the pain that you cause,
Or maybe in haste,
You neglected to pause,
You unburdened yourself,
Without thought or ill will,
But a soul is now suffering,
From your bitter pill.

Has truth to be always,
A statement of fact?
Or should it be subject,
To thought and to tact?

The Waterfall of Life

Should it always be open,
For public approval,
Once out of the bag,
It precludes its removal.

Words hurt like stones,
When rumours abound,
And can hurt just as much,
If you believe they are sound!

The half-truths, and fake truths,
Like wildfire are spread,
But you know they are evil,
You have been misled.

August 28, 2017

Coming Of Age

Is it true said the child to its father,
That we all have to be very good,
And we don't have a choice if we'd rather,
Be naughty and play in the mud?

The father was pensive and thoughtful,
And pondered this question some time.
If you want to be naughty then do it my child,
I still will upbraid you, but it will only be mild.

You have a will of your own, and you must be free,
To find your own path, without advice from me,
I always will be here, you can on that, depend,
And your independent rights, I strongly, will defend."

The child looked up, and shaking her head,
That is not good guidance, father, she said,
I need to know the wrong, from the right,
The difference is all, be it, ever so slight.

You sought my advice, and that I have given,
your words show, down what path you are driven,
I cannot do better than where you are now,
Your admonishment proves you already know how!

September 27, 2017

Out Of Time

Go not to where the grogwarts go,
Where the fanged tooth ratgut bites,
Where death is rife and life is cheap,
And they practise pagan rites.

A throwback to pre-history,
It is a place of shadows and mystery,
It is hidden in the dark of the woods,
guarded by hobgoblins in hoods.

This infestation in ancient days,
Was kept in order by Druid ways,
Who would gather at the full of the moon,
Sacrificing chickens, and chanting songs till noon.

The beasts are free to roam and kill,
you can hear their awful howling still,
They are, atop, of that far rocky hill,
fighting each other and growling.

It is here that the evil wolverine lurk,
Preying on innocents, going to work,
They now will face his merciless wrath,
Having strayed from the normal quite safe path,

For centuries now this evil place,
Has kept, its anonymity safe,
An anomaly, in space and time,
Has opened a door, to this world of slime.

How is this possible with modern techniques,
That no one has noticed these terrible freaks?
You can try and avoid a confrontation,
But something should be done, by the leaders of the nation.

October 14, 2017

Water

Rain on the rocks and the heather on high,
Fall on the mountain from a dark clouded sky,
Myriad droplets create pools of reflection,
Then stream all together in a downward direction.

It wends its way through rill and gully,
It babbles and scrabbles, in hectic hurry,
It soon is a river flowing and wide,
With fields and meadows on either side.

It ambles, now no need for haste,
Meandering its way at a leisurely pace,
It swirls and whirls, as it joins with the flow,
Embracing an estuary in a wanton show.

Water finds its level, wherever it may be,
Eventually it ends up back into the sea,
The sea turns to clouds and then to rain,
So the original stream, lives, to stream again.

November 29, 2017

Damian Cranney

Parky Benders

Are all things purposeful and sane,
What in this life have we to gain,
Of telling others how we feel?
Illness makes life seem surreal.

I have not spoken of the time,
My time was less than I thought due,
Having Parkinson's I thought a crime,
Because it cut my time with you.

Ten years have passed, the time just flew
I put it all down to loving you,
My need was great, but you were there,
Giving me love as well as care.

Some people fight to win a war,
or fight the neighbours just next door,
We have fought the P. together,
at this rate I should last forever.

December 9, 2017

The Strength Within

I have walked through fields of doubt,
I have driven across arid plains,
I have swum the rivers of life,
And still, hope eternal, remains.

Never yield to the frailness without,
It is the strength within that shapes us,
There are no negatives, only inaction,
Climb your own mountain, trigger reaction.

Age and sickness are not the same,
You can be young, and not be sound,
You can be old, and not be lame,
You can be both, yet be unbound.

Do not write me off just yet,
My intentions are not to go,
In fields of passion I still walk,
And may it ever be so.

January 21, 2018

Damian Cranney

Free Moments In Time

I am grateful,

for having been granted,

this life, such as it may be,

The simplest of things,

still make me enchanted,

but I know there's much more,

than the little I see.

A new born child,

grips your finger,

with tiny baby hands,

And later when it smiles,

and shows it understands,

That you will always be there,

no matter what befalls,

And when the child becomes adult,

it's that moment one recalls.

Life is made up,

of moments like these,

So is there a price,

you must pay for it please?

You have to give,

The Waterfall of Life

before you can take,
And it's yourself that you give,
and for your own sake.

The sum of all happiness,
is human interaction,
But the only way it works,
is if it's selfless benefaction,
If aims are materialistic,
your rewards you will receive,
But happiness it will not buy,
do not yourself deceive.

February 22, 2018

Damian Cranney

Peace On Earth

In a corner of France is a gravestone,
'An Unknown Soldier' the only tribute shown,
It represents all of the fallen brave,
Who fell like skittles, in that stark enclave.

The Victoria Cross, the Croix De Guerre,
The Iron Cross, and the Lenin Bear,
Symbols awarded in the absurdity of war,
To encourage and nurture an Espri du Corps.

The dead who lie in long straight rows,
Are indifferent now to the rhetoric and prose,
Urged to fight others who were just like them,
Only to end up as anonymous dead men.

Why is our future in the hands of a few,
Who ignore the lessons of the historical view?
Power in their hands will cause chaos and rupture,
Building the blocks that will destroy all our future.

The world stage is full, of leaders acting macho,
Strutting the boards like mannequins in panto,
They play with the lives of the peoples of this planet,
Peace should be their aim, if only they would plan it.

April 1, 2018

Shield Of Truth

I am lost in the darkness,
Blind to the light,
Struggling to find my way,
in this stygian night.

I know that there is somewhere,
A place prepared for me,
But my wanderings have not revealed,
What my destiny will be.

The world is spinning freely,
There is no one at the helm,
Gyrating wildly like a top,
Into a darker realm.

Send someone to guide me,
Is heaven that far away?
Where is my guardian angel,
To teach me how to pray?

If there is a God, then show me,
Let me see his face,
Give me understanding,
Help me moderate my pace.

I saw the sun this morning,
It warmed my heart to see,
A new day now was dawning
With the freedom to be free.

Truth is all that matters,
In that you must not yield,
Keep it always by your side,
And it will be your shield.

July 3, 2019

Steam Travel

Steam Trains, are archaic,
Romantic and prosaic.
It takes an army of volunteers
to keep these old trains going.
What will happen, in the future?
There is just no way of knowing,

To go by train,
on a summer's day out,
Hoping that it would not rain,
Was, what a day out, was all about.

Boiled egg sandwiches,
A flask full of tea,
Balanced precariously,
Upon your knee.

When I was young,
the journey made,
Was, from Temple Meads to the arcade,
Along the front,
At Weston-super-Mare,
Ice cream and rock,
With friends to share.

Damian Cranney

We all have memories,
just like these,
It was easy then,
For us to please,
The donkey rides,
The puppet show,
Ice cream and,
lemonade to go,
A sunny day out,
drinking in the shade.

Time to go home,
And the platform is chocker,
To get on the train,
You need the build of a docker,
With the smoke from the steam,
And the noise from the wheels,
To remind you just,
How that moment feels.

Gradually you start to move,
Two short blasts,
And the train starts to roll,
The sounds and smells,
Are written in your soul,

The Waterfall of Life

with the rat tat tat,
And the clickety click,
Of the train on the track,
You are on your way back.
Home is not too far away,
And you can put your feet up,
At the end of the day.

January 31, 2020

Damian Cranney

Agincourt

Bowman, thou art fit and strong,
Armed with a bow, six foot long,
A weapon made, for war and death,
Defend the right, till your last breath.

Draw me an arrow, straight and long,
Aim it at that motley throng,
There stands our forsworn enemy,
Fighting, like us, to be free.

The odds are six to one, my friend,
But that did not matter in the end,
Thirty thousand made a stance,
Fighting for their king and France.

They faced six thousand men of war
Led by a king, whose cause was sure,
Bowmen from the Hills of Wales,
Yeomen from the English Vales.

The thirty thousand French were brave,
But the charge they made, was to the grave,
On muddied ground, beneath a blackened sky,
They died by thousands, in a field of Rye.

The Waterfall of Life

A bowman's rate of fire, is great,
Ten arrows per minute they estimate,
At Agincourt five thousand men,
Released a quarter of a million then.

That was the day that chivalry died,
Honour was challenged and defied,
So many prisoners could not be left,
To challenge their rear and leave them bereft.

Henry would not take the bond,
That prisoners would not abscond,
He put them to the sword, to die,
Ten thousand on that bloody field, still lie.

Henry was English, a pragmatic King,
Chivalry is pointless, if you lose everything,
He won the war, without disgrace,
England now was a safer place.

Bowman thou art fit and strong,
Armed with a bow, six foot long,
A weapon made, for war and death,
Defend the right, till your last breath.

April 14, 2020

Damian Cranney

Excuse For War

Think of the man,
Imprisoned for his faith,
Think of the dead,
who no longer have a face.

Neither can alter,
Their future or their fate,
Many of us may falter,
before reaching heaven's gate.

Ponder on the refugee,
Deemed to have no right,
Dwell on the suffering,
Of innocents in flight.

Condemned by yet another war,
Forced to leave their home,
It has happened, many times before,
They all are forced to roam.

Children, mothers, babies,
With nowhere else to run,
Crippled, dead, or dying,
By the bomb, or by the gun.

The Waterfall of Life

Our countries make those weapons,
Can we justify our role?
They sear the flesh of all our sons,
And blast our very soul.

We salve the guilt, by saying,
We cannot be held to account,
We don't count the dead or dying,
Only the fiscal amount.

It was not us, who pulled the trigger?
Well, that is a feeble excuse,
Go tell that to the graveyard digger,
Who buries the bodies, from war's abuse.

May 2, 2020

Damian Cranney

A Buzzing Bee

I saw a busy bumblebee,
Grazing on the dew,
It buzzed from flower to flower,
Of red white and blue.

Collecting golden nectar
from the stem of every bud,
which one day would be honey,
at least I think it should.

The sky was an azure blue,
Below the fields were green,
The clouds were white as snow,
Reflected in a nearby stream.

It was peaceful,
And yet the woods all around,
Was noisy and calming,
With nature's wonderful sound.

I walked down a track,
Back to the car,
Someone had left the gates all ajar,
Very naughty I thought to myself.

The Waterfall of Life

There were sheep,
And a farmer mad as a judge,
Because all of his sheep,
just would not budge.

It did not take him long to rally,
And the head count,
Also seemed to tally,
The baby lambs were bleating,
I used a nearby rock for seating.

What a wonderful life
we have in nature!
Next time I think,
I'll take the wife,
This place could do,
with a little strife.

July 7, 2020

Rabbit

I went out shooting rabbits,
And had a very, very good day,
It's becoming a bit of a habit,
This going out to shoot rabbit.

If you want to feed your family,
It's your duty and you must,
They will eat fried rabbit happily,
With a piece of bread and a crust.

However they will not eat,
What appears to be, a cute little bunny,
You can cook it however you like,
You can cook it with herbs and with honey.

As long as it doesn't look like a pet,
You may as well stay at home with the vet,
Gut it and dress it, so it looks quite bland,
As if you had bought it, in a shop, from a stand.

Kids nowadays appear quite alarming,
they are not aware of traditional farming,
cocooned from birth in a nanny state,
Not aware of how meat arrives on their plate.

The Waterfall of Life

The journey of life, from the farm to the table,
Is taken for granted, by those that are able,
That juicy steak eaten with relish,
Spent time on the hoof, to improve and embellish.

It did not run round fields,
Disguised as a vacuum pack,
It was probably a handsome steer,
Processed into a plastic bag.

June 27, 2021

Damian Cranney

Duel Of Death

The coldness of the night had passed,
The light was set, the die was cast,
A pair of mortals faced each other,
Neither thinking of his mother.

Each with an evil glint in his eye,
Each one determined the other would die,
One man weak and one man strong,
Each one certain the other was wrong.

Two men gaunt and two men true,
stood beside as seconds do,
One advanced and with a nod,
Placed pistols chassied upon the sod.

Below amid the darkened trees,
As heaven creates a silent breeze,
A frail and fretful figure stands,
Her heart was twisting like her hands.

Two guns long in fists of might,
Two guns aimed at death in sight,
Over the rims they saw each other,
Man to man and brother to brother.

The Waterfall of Life

A mother's heart was pensive still,
Could she stop this deadly skill?
When each soul was bent upon,
Destruction of the other one.

The master of the duel grim,
Whose face was set, whose eyes were dim,
He raised his hand aloft on high,
Until it almost reached the sky.

The debt to mother love he'd pay,
If he could stop this deadly fray,
But now the pennant white was drawn,
The hope of rescue was forlorn.

It poised and then to earth it fell,
To cast a sinner down to hell,
Each player poised on bated breath,
A trigger squeeze and then came death.

It hit the taller of the two,
The bullet to his heart it flew,
Out from his lips there came a groan,
And from the trees a dreadful moan.

The mother to her knees did fall,
And knelt beside her young son Paul,
Grief stricken with the thought of him,
Who had done this to his next of kin.

The slayer now with head low bent,
Whose heart was torn, whose soul was rent,
Advanced pace towards his brother,
And gazed with sadness on his mother.

With loving gaze and tender touch,
Knowing that she'd suffered much,
the son who triumphed over death,
Looked down at her with bated breath.

She turned and looked at him with hate,
He who had made his brother's fate,
And picking up the unfired gun,
She aimed, killed her other son.

His look no pity could impart,
And it passed heavy o'er her heart,
Across his brother's corpse he fell,
And Satan claimed two more for hell.

The mother now for murder stood,
    Upon a gallows made of wood,
A hangman's noose, for her was made,
    Justice for her crime was paid.

August 5, 2021

Damian Cranney

The Undefeated

Tyson Fury, he's a man,
If he says he'll do it, you know he can,
He has been down, but never beaten,
He can never be accused of cheatin'

He has risen like the Pheonix,
Many times before,
His battles have been many,
But he finally won the War.

His biggest fight is with himself,
He is both, Protagonist and Referee,
He will not be left upon the shelf,
His inner fight has set him free.

He is an inspiration,
To all of those who share,
A lack of motivation,
Or a need for special care.

Cassius Clay, aka Mohammed Ali,
Did rather well, like Tyson Fury,
His biggest fight, was a neuron disease,
Parkinson's does not leave one at ease.

The Waterfall of Life

There were times Tyson felt rejected,
Not understood, or respected,
But a new Tyson Fury was unfurled,
Retiring undefeated, 'Champion of the World'.

April 27, 2022

Damian Cranney

Take No Care For Tomorrow

Here's to those who have gone before,
And to those we hope will follow,
There are those who journey stoically,
While others find life a bore.

Do not forget the gift of life,
Is something we all borrow,
Live every day as if you know,
There won't be a tomorrow.

Each of us is different,
And yet we are all the same,
Life has many paths to take,
Just treat it like a game.

And like a game, it doesn't matter,
If you win or lose,
But then again, it's better,
If the winning path you choose.

And when you're at the finish,
And they've totted up your place,
If you have fully loved and lived,
You know you've won the race.

November 11, 2022

One Man's War

This War Should End
The Lubianka doors clanged loudly,
As the soldier turned the key,
Young Putin strode out proudly,
He had just joined the KGB.

On his way to destiny,
And all the many deaths,
Do you think he would know,
Would anyone guess?

That, we all will die,
Because of him,
And know, he couldn't care less,
His humanity replaced, by personal success.

Who would have thought that in this human time,
When history tells us, what a war will do,
Someone with short term gain will risk,
Ten billion human souls, to fulfil his wish?

Putin, we call upon you,
To stop this carnage now,
Or is your heart so callous,
Or is your soul so dead?

Damian Cranney

Or is it, that your pride
won't let you, 'Say you were not right'?
Do not worry, right is might,
And that young mother with her kids,

Will thank you forever.
Come on do it, end this disgusting fight
You always put yourself in front, others never,
Stopping this war is the only claim that's clever.

Where have all the wise men gone?

Where have all the wise men gone,
Those sages who in times long past,
Would tell us what we need do,
To make our collective dreams come true?

There are no sages to be found,
To make us respect this hallowed ground,
Lessons from the past,
No longer are respected.

Unfettered greed, and infinite ambition,
Political need, and existential aggression,
All married together, in autocratic delusion,
The end of the world will be its conclusion.

The world does need changing,
But the question is by who,
It has to be, by men of good will,
Whose humanity shines through.

Starting a war is a silly idea,

It means you've not learnt,

The lessons of the past,

and are destined to repeat, The mistakes that will last.

April 2, 2023

Daniel Cretona

Poor old Daniel Cretona,
He carries the woes of the world on his shoulder,
He remembers when young, fearing total destruction,
As there seemed no chance for peaceful construction.

The fears disappeared in the following years,
There seemed now no need to shed any tears,
The cold in the east seemed to warm to the west,
The bear its aggression it appeared to divest.

But then what followed, was a world badly led,
The olive Branches on offer are all now dead,
The Stars and the Stripes, puffed its chest with delight,
Thinking they had won the long cold fight.

And instead of taking the bear by the hand,
And creating for all a new promised land,
Gave no respect to the state of the bear,
Left it brooding and angry, alone in its lair.

This earth needs something better than this,
If you ask me our leaders, we all should dismiss,
They haven't a clue on What they should do,
They should just leave it to me and to you.

June 2013